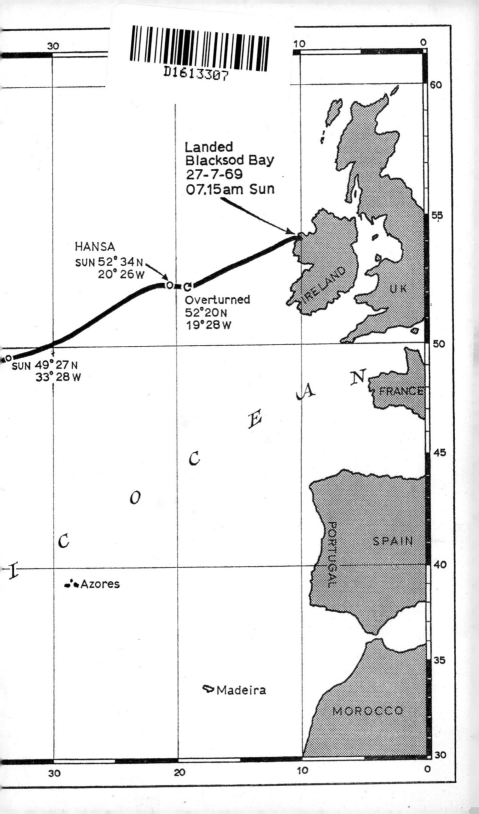

Landed
Blacksod Bay
27-7-69
07.15am Sun

HANSA
SUN 52°34 N
20°26 W

Overturned
52°20 N
19°28 W

SUN 49°27 N
33°28 W

IRELAND

UK

FRANCE

N

E

A

C

C

O

C

I

PORTUGAL

SPAIN

Azores

Madeira

MOROCCO

I HAD TO DARE

Rowing the Atlantic in Seventy Days

Tom McClean

I HAD TO DARE

Rowing the Atlantic in Seventy Days

JARROLDS, LONDON

JARROLDS PUBLISHERS (LONDON) LTD
3 Fitzroy Square, London W1

 AN IMPRINT OF THE HUTCHINSON GROUP

London Melbourne Sydney Auckland
Wellington Johannesburg Cape Town
and agencies throughout the world

First published 1971

*This book has been set in Baskerville type, printed in Great Britain
on antique wove paper by Anchor Press, and
bound by Wm. Brendon, both of Tiptree, Essex*

ISBN 0 09 108680 9

Acknowledgements

My thanks are due to Peter Vane of the *Sunday Express* for his help in preparing this book and to all the other people without whose assistance this adventure would not have been possible.

Contents

Illustrations

I | The reason why
10-17 May

There was nothing but snow and ice below me. It seemed as if the entire world was made of the stuff. It spread to the north, to the south, to the east and the west as far as the eye could see and beyond. Mile upon mile of it, glaring, dazzling, shimmering in pale spring sunshine and, on every horizon, imperceptibly merging into a smoky blue sky.

I had to shut my eyes. Spots, red, orange and blue, jigged behind my closed eyelids. But I had to look again. Never before had I seen such a vast wasteland of lifelessness. Nothing but still, chilling whiteness like some monumental TV commercial for a soap powder. There was nothing to see except long jagged cracks in the surface where water and wind had combined, and failed, to break up the huge mass. Nothing moved. Not even a shadow. I felt as if I was stepping back, back, back to the very dawn of time itself.

I hunched forward in the seat of the RAF Comet and wondered: 'What the hell have I let myself in for?'

As I watched, an RAF corporal on his way to join the air station at Goose Bay, Newfoundland, nudged me and said: 'Tom, if it's like that all the way across you'll just have to get your skates out.'

He was half serious, half joking. But those few words broke a slight tension which had been building up inside me. I readily joined the rest of the passengers in their laughter.

It is at moments like these that one wonders if laughing is the correct thing to do. Would it, to the rest of them in the plane, sound like bravado, nerves or just sheer stupidity? Maybe it was a mixture of all three. Everyone on board knew why I was sitting there in that RAF transport. I was on my way to St Johns, Newfoundland—the starting point I had chosen for my single-handed row across the Atlantic.

I had hoped to be the first man to start and complete a lone

Atlantic row. But John Fairfax was already in the water and heading for America. I just had to beat him across. I am a competitive sort of character and competition needs some motivating force. It can be the tearing airless hollow in your chest which urges you on to be first at the tape or drop in the attempt. It can be the challenge of someone behind you, someone close, so close you hear them breathing down your neck.

But here was a man I had never seen, thousands of miles away and already rowing while I was preparing to fly to St Johns. Every delay, every hour away from the start of my row, grew more and more intolerable. I sealed off a corner of my mind and blamed John Fairfax. It has been said that a good fighter has to be full of either hunger or hate. I began to hate John Fairfax.

It helped. It gave me the sense of urgency I needed. Now it is all over I apologise to John and say: 'Thanks for the help.'* But I couldn't blame John for that sea of ice I saw from the plane. In fact I didn't even think of him. We were somewhere just south of the Arctic Circle. It was 10 May. I had expected to find some ice still hanging around, but it shook me to see it there so far south and looking solid enough never to melt in a year of summers. And I felt sure that it must stretch all the way to the harbour of St Johns.

I remember thinking: 'It's going to be damn' cold.' That's all. Funny how one's mind centres mainly on what can physically be seen at a given moment. Winds, storms, towering seas were far from my mind. I was mentally checking over my warm clothing. Would I have enough? Would it be the right sort of equipment?

Looking back, it all seems a needless worry. But I shan't forget it. I will not forget anything that happened during that voyage. My little twenty-foot-long Yorkshire-built dory *Super Silver* and I were up to our gunwales and neck in a fight that

* John Fairfax, in fact, landed only a few days ahead of me. Rowing from east to west and using the Canary Islands as his starting point, Fairfax's twenty-two-foot-long mahogany-built *Britannia* slid on to Hollywood Beach in Florida after a crossing which had taken 180 days.

He had, during that time, taken on fresh food and water supplies from passing ships. He stepped ashore on 20 July 1969, almost exactly one week before I landed in Northern Ireland.

lasted seventy days and seventeen hours practically without let-up.

Of course, there were moments of calm, moments of blissful peace when aching bones and blistered backside found sheer luxury by wallowing in stinking sea water rippling across the floorboards of *Super Silver*. But at other times, when the sea seemed alive with fury, when fog clammily shrouded broad daylight in twilight mystery, when my feet seemed as if they would drop off from frostbite, when a singularly single-minded shark shadowed me for days and when the wind seemed to be howling for my blood—I'll admit it, I was scared. So scared I prayed.

Yet I've not had a sleepless night since that voyage. No nightmares, not even the whisper of a dream about it. But I will always remember. Like an ageing lover who can recall the vital statistics of his old flames; like an old soldier who chews over old battles and once again smells the excitement, the danger, the sheer exhilaration of being alive when the smoke has cleared, my Atlantic memories will remain etched, crystal clear, on my mind for ever.

Before I left, and since my return, most people want to know 'Why?' To many of them it must have seemed a stupid caper. An aimless adventure. Indeed, some have said straight out: 'You're either stark, staring mad or nothing more than a show-off.'

I don't think I'm crazy. And I certainly don't think of my-self as a hero. It was simply that I wanted to achieve something. I wanted to amount to something. I wanted to make my mark. I did know, however, that one day I would find the answer.

I'm Dublin-born of Irish parents, so I have a streak of stubbornness. Although fiercely proud of my Irish heritage, I am now a British citizen and proud of that too. Pride alone, however, is not enough to bring success.

It was very early in life that I faced up to the indisputable fact that I just didn't have what it takes to be a Prime Minister, an industrial tycoon or a Nobel Prize winner. I was woefully short on glitter when it came to some sort of stardom. Come to that, for most of my early years I was also short of common sense.

I was orphaned at the age of three and at the English orphan-age where I grew up there were some pretty tough lads. I thought them a bundle of fun at the time. The truth is, if I hadn't joined the Army I would have ended up as a Teddy Boy and who knows what from there? When it did dawn on me the answer was startlingly clear. You may not have much in the way of cash, background or education, but make use of what you *have* got—youth, extreme fitness, strength and an un-quenchable yen for adventure.

Funnily enough, I was nowhere near the sea when the idea of rowing the Atlantic first took shape. I was deep in the Borneo jungle serving with the Parachute Regiment during the days of the British confrontation with the Indonesian Communists who were threatening Malaya. The nearest water was the stuff bubbling away in the dixie ready for a quick brew-up. We were resting in a small clearing as fresh supplies were parachuted in to us. Amongst those supplies were some three-week-old news-papers. I settled down with a cup of char and opened one of the papers. I couldn't believe it. There, staring me in the face, was a picture of my old paratrooper pals John Ridgway and Chay Blyth. They were grinning like mad.

It said they were going to attempt rowing the Atlantic in a twenty-three-foot Yorkshire dory. 'Blimey,' I thought, 'what a great caper!' I couldn't get them out of my head. I thought about them all morning. I was still thinking about them as we swung off on jungle patrol. 'If they can pull that off,' I thought, 'they will really have done something worth while.'

That was early in 1966. I was back in England by the time they pushed off from a beach near Cape Cod, Massachusetts, in June that year. I followed their progress across the Atlantic almost inch by inch. Every report was read and re-read. I was at London Airport when they made their triumphant return to add my congratulations to the rest from all over the world.

A few months later a bunch of us were chatting about Ridgway and Blyth in the barrack room at the Special Air Service HQ at Hereford.

I suddenly said: 'I reckon one person could do it.'

Even now I don't really know what prompted me to say that. I had not made a study of a lone row. I hadn't thought about it in any detail. I don't think I had even thought of myself attempting it. Suddenly, however, I felt positive it could be done.

A couple of my chums laughed. 'Belt up, Moby,' they said. 'You're bats. It took Blyth and Ridgway all their time to do it together, and, as they've already told us, it was no picnic.'

I didn't argue. I didn't say I would, or could, row the Atlantic alone. I just repeated: 'I think one person could do it.'

From that day I began the long preparation without having any clear idea of what to do or even that I would do it. I sent off to the Admiralty chartmakers for charts of the Atlantic Ocean and the Irish and British coasts. And I burned up the telephone wires with inquiry calls to boatbuilders.

The firm supplying the charts could not understand why a SAS man should want such detailed information about the Atlantic. I don't know what they thought about it. They never told me and I never had a chance to ask. To say the least, they must have thought it damned odd. At the most serious they probably believed it possible that some breach of security was involved. Or maybe they figured I was planning to desert. Whatever their reasons, they reported the matter to the SAS authorities.

The first I knew about the concern I had innocently aroused came with a sharp summons to appear before Major Dodds, my squadron commander. 'Now then, McClean,' he barked, 'what's all this business with charts?'

My mind was made up in a flash. At last I really knew what had been pushing me, urging me for the past months. I knew what I wanted to do. My brain raced with all my old dreams of making good; of amounting to something; of achieving something which would make my life worth while. I was still breathless with the whole idea as I heard myself reply: 'I want to row the Atlantic, sir.'

'Alone?' curtly asked Major Dodds.

'Yes, sir.' I didn't say that I wanted to be the *first* man to do it alone. But that was the vital point. Two men, Ridgway and Blyth, had done it together. Two others, David Johnstone and John Hoare, had perished in a two-man attempt, and Fairfax, although he may well have been making his preparations, had not been heard of by the general public. I figured I had a good clear run. Anybody who could make that first lone Atlantic row would be chalking up an all-world record.

I nearly burst out laughing as I watched Major Dodds's face. I remember thinking of the remark on my SAS training report when I was accepted for the unit: 'Has a tendency to talk before he thinks.' Had I done it again? Not to worry. I didn't care if I had. This was finally what my life was all about. I knew it deep down in my bones.

Major Dodds finally spoke. He carefully looked over my five feet six inches—I was one of the shortest men in the regiment—and slowly said: 'You're mad, McClean. Are you absolutely sure? Do you realise just what such a project would entail?'

I just said: 'Yes, sir,' once again. And Major Dodds said: 'All right, I'll get you an interview with the CO.'

A few weeks later in 1967 I was wheeled into the office of the CO, Colonel John Slim, son of Field Marshal Sir William Slim of World War II fame. He was great. He didn't preach. He didn't enthuse. He just asked, with great deliberation: 'Are you absolutely sure that you want to tackle this?'

'Yes, sir,' I replied. Fleetingly I thought I didn't seem to be contributing much to these conversations except those two words. I didn't need to.

'Right,' said Colonel Slim. 'First I want you to find out exactly what sort of boat you want. Then have a shot at rowing a boat for a few hours. Then have a talk with Ridgway and Blyth and get their firm opinions on your chances.'

I believed then, and still do, that Colonel Slim was testing me out to make sure that I really knew what I was taking on. Fair enough. I went right ahead.

I caught a train down to the Isle of Wight and, hiring a row-boat, put in a stint of eight hours. That, apart from an odd splash on the Serpentine, was the most rowing I had ever done in my life. Basically I knew nothing about rowing, but that was something I had to keep to myself. If that had been made public, people really would have thought me utterly crazy. That Isle of Wight practice was nothing like rowing the Atlantic, of course. It gave me no inkling at all of what lay ahead. I'm glad now that it did not. But at least it confirmed what I already knew. My muscles were capable of standing long hours of severe physical effort without any serious effect.

When I visited Ridgway at his croft-based adventure school in the Scottish Highlands I found him somewhat dubious about my chances. Looking back, I am sure poor old Ridge was on the horns of a dilemma. Quite obviously he did not want to discourage me. Yet, at the same time, he did not want to feel himself responsible in any way for urging me into a foolhardy venture which might end in my death. And I'm sure that is how he privately felt I would end my grand adventure.

That, I suppose, is one of the difficulties of having officer training. I reckon he felt himself responsible for the well-being of one of his men. You cannot shake off that sense of duty after being in the Army for several years.

Cautiously he advised: 'Quite honestly, Tom, I don't think one man could do it. There were times when Chay and I did not think we would be able to make it together. There is really no way of describing briefly the incredible number of emergencies which can suddenly overtake you out there. And there is no way of advising how to cope with them except to say you just have to stick it out.'

Then we chatted over Atlantic seamanship and Ridge was enormously helpful. His last words were: 'I would estimate that you will need about three years to get ready if you decide to go ahead.'

I was not feeling nearly so bouncy on the train back to London. Ridge had pointed out some very valid details which I had only vaguely comprehended until then. I realised then how vital it was that they should have been laid on the line for me. His estimation of three years' preparation had also dampened me quite a bit. Now that I had really made up my mind I wanted to get on with the job as soon as possible.

I watched the countryside whizzing by and caught a glimpse of myself in the carriage window. My face had set in heavy brooding lines. I shook myself, grinned at my reflection—thank goodness the carriage was empty—and told myself: 'Phooey. Three years be blowed. That is far too long. I'll find some way of cutting the time.'

My next stop was Chay Blyth's home near Portsmouth. His

B

pretty wife Maureen listened silently as we chatted. I shot a glance at her now and then and couldn't help thinking: 'Here is the girl who waited without a murmur while Chay was thirteen weeks in the Atlantic. She's got a lot of guts but I wonder how she really felt about it all?'

Chay himself was full of enthusiasm. He was also absolutely blunt. 'It's a great idea, Tom,' he told me. 'But I want to make it quite clear to you that you are taking on a hell of a handful. I won't beat about the bush. . . . I reckon you have an 80–20 chance of success.'

He stopped talking and just looked at me. I didn't say a word. I just nodded. Chay waited a little longer, grinned and said: 'OK, let's get down to cases and see how we can really help you.'

We talked for hours and I made notes. Chay's advice was invaluable. As I left Maureen kissed me lightly on the cheek and said: 'Goodbye, Tom, and good luck.' For the first time I realised just how lucky I was to be a loner. I wondered how much my determination would have been affected if I had been married. I wondered what sort of personal agony Chay and Ridge must have gone through when they first talked over their Atlantic plans with their wives. With no wife, not even a steady girl friend, and no close relations I thanked my lucky stars I was completely free of any chance of emotional upsets.

Two weeks after seeing Colonel Slim I was back in his office with a report of my preliminary plans for the trip. There were no more questions. The Colonel wrote off to the War Office asking permission for me to make the row. It was granted. The Army was magnificent. I was told I would be given paid leave while I made my preparations and unpaid leave to make the row itself. The Army was also prepared to help me in any way possible within the terms of its own commitments as a body which is paid by the taxpayers.

By this time it was nearing Christmas 1968. Deciding on what sort of boat to use was simple. What had served Ridgway and Blyth so well could surely not be bettered. And both of them had spoken highly of the little and flimsy-looking craft built by Bradford Boat Services of Yorkshire. I ordered one, three feet shorter than *English Rose III*, and things really began to get a move on. There were, however, still a multitude of details to think of. The most important was money.

I had enough in my savings to pay out £200 for the boat. Where was the rest to come from? I estimated I would need about £3,000 all told if I had to pay for everything. An ordinary soldier just does not have that sort of loot. I needed special clothing, food supplies, navigational instruments, oars, pumps . . . it seemed like a never-ending list.

My worries did not last long. Kind-hearted people who had heard of my plans by this time began rallying round. Mr John Colam, a Herefordshire businessman, paid for three sets of special oars and workmen in his factory made a cylindrical metal shield to protect my camping-style gas cooker from the wind. They also made a watertight metal box to guard my radio from the salt air. Tesco, the supermarket chain, donated a stock of 'goodies'—tins of jam, fruit, pots of curry paste, chocolate, etc. Whitbread, the brewers, threw in cans of beer and Kinlochs gave me some bottles of rum.

On the advice of Chay Blyth I had taken on an agent, ex-Fleet Street journalist Paul Sargent. It seemed no time at all before other firms were also offering help. Waterproof watches, a chronometer, a two-way radio, a life-jacket with emergency radio attached, all came flowing in. Some were on loan. Some were given free of charge. And I made an advertising agreement with most of the firms dependent on whether my row was successful.

I will admit that although I was not making the trip for sheer financial gain I was interested in making it pay if I could. For by the time it was all over I would have finished my time in the Army and I felt that I would be better equipped to face civilian life if I had a stake. I was thinking in terms of enough to start myself in some sort of small business. Just enough to avoid having to take a 9 am to 5 pm job which after service life would have been a drudge.

Benefiting from the experience of Ridgway and Blyth, I did not attempt to persuade a national newspaper to sponsor my trip. Quite understandably no newspaper wants to finance what could turn out to be a disaster. Even more important, from their point of view, most newspapers do not like encouraging somebody to do something which at first sight seems thoroughly foolhardy.

Paul and I decided to try the matter on a different tack. We would not ask for outright support but instead suggest that payment be made *if* the trip was successful. We decided to approach the *Sunday Express* which has always had a fundamental interest in adventure. I had a long interview with Peter Vane, the chief reporter and an ex-Royal Navy man. I think he was frankly horrified when I told him I had practically no rowing experience; had never handled a row-boat in heavy seas; knew nothing at all about seamanship and that my navigational talents were limited to my land map-reading courses with the Army.

Not once did he reveal what he really thought. I still have no idea what he reported back to his office. Finally there were a couple of meetings with him and the news and features editors. Eventually a contract was drawn up on the basis of buying my log of the trip and any photographs I took so long as I was successful. The first part of the contract allowed for my making it to roughly the halfway stage and then, for whatever reason, perhaps having to give up. The second part, covering double payment, allowed for my making it all the way.

By the middle of April 1969 I was beginning to feel as ready as I ever would be. The hull of *Super Silver* was propped up on rubber pads in the carpenters' shop at SAS headquarters at Hereford. The Army had allowed me the help of one of the base chippies (carpenters) and we had almost completed the modifications needed on the boat.

We had built five-foot-long buoyancy compartments fore and aft. They were made of tough marine plywood and turtle-decked on the top. Inside the compartments were stuffed to choking point with blocks of polystyrene. When the time came eighty gallons of drinking water (1,200 lb in weight) would be distributed evenly under *Super Silver*'s floorboards as a counter-balance, the theory being that, if the boat capsized, the weight of the drinking water would tend to twist downwards and the buoyancy blocks upwards, thus righting the boat. And I am convinced now that my life was saved by that wonderful mixture of polystyrene and drinking water.

Those two buoyancy compartments left exactly ten feet of open space in *Super Silver*. Following my talks with Ridgway and Blyth, I decided to make it even smaller. They had no shelter at all on their dory. Their main protection against the weather had been Army rubberised poncho capes. And they suffered.

From the bulkhead of the after compartment I built out a slightly curved plywood canopy about three feet long and stretching from gunwale to gunwale. The front was left completely open. Under the canopy I had a space measuring two feet seven inches at its highest centre point, about four feet wide and three feet long. It was not, however, all for me. I planned that it should also act as a shelter for such precious items as the chronometer, radios, perishable foods and the inflatable rubber dinghy loaned to me by the RAF.

So much for my pathetically puny plans. By the second day out the damp, the salt and the freezing cold had penetrated to every corner of that little space. For when the crunch came there was not enough room for my air bed . . . the one touch of luxury I had allowed myself. I had to lay it fore and aft leaving about three feet of it sticking out in the open. I decided I would just have to make the best of it. At that stage I had not even thought of the possibility of frostbite attacking my feet until they were so swollen that I wouldn't be able to wear boots for days on end.

One of my remaining worries, enough main food supplies to last the hundred days I calculated I would be at sea, was cleared up by the Army. They supplied me with 100 SAS field ration packs. Each one contains enough calories, in mostly dehydrated form, to keep a hard-working man going all day.

The days were spinning by now. I estimated that, all being well, I should be able to start rowing from St Johns on 10 May. I had chosen St Johns quite deliberately as my starting point. Ridgway and Blyth had started from the Massachusetts coast which gave them better climatic conditions but they admitted to me that an awful lot of precious time was wasted as prevalent winds first swept them on a mainly northerly course instead of towards the British Isles. I knew full well the hazards of the more northerly course I had chosen. It would be that much

colder and more uncomfortable. It would also include the
hazards of floating pack-ice and icebergs.

But it had one great and vital advantage. At St Johns the
Newfoundland coast juts well out into the Atlantic. It is, in
effect, the shortest distance between the coastline of the north
American continent and that of the British Isles. I had estimated it on the charts as 2,058 miles. With luck, kindly winds,
and a bit more luck, I should be able to make it.

Super Silver was already waiting for me at St Johns as the RAF
Comet winged its way over the ice and snow fields below the
Arctic Circle. The Furness Withy shipping company had shipped it over free of charge, together with all my supplies, a couple
of weeks earlier. I was looking forward to seeing little *Silver*
once again.

Although I had planned to set sail on 10 May, due to various
small but time-consuming hold-ups it was not until that day
that I actually arrived at St Johns. I was behind schedule and
I didn't like it. There was nothing to do, however, except to
get cracking as soon as possible. That was not too easy in a place
like St Johns.

My arrival caused quite a stir, for the Newfoundland fishermen are some of the finest dory-boat handlers in the world.
Although they plainly thought of me as some sort of oddity they
were far too polite to actually say so. In fact I worried at first
that their overwhelming kindness would delay my departure
yet further. There were invitations to dinner, to lunch, to
homes, to car rides, to parties, to drinks. I thought they would
swamp me with their kindness. Luckily I am no drinker and
was able quite truthfully to refuse the mountainous offers of
alcoholic refreshments. If I had accepted just half of them I
reckon I would have had to go through a dehydration course
before ever attempting to set sail.

The Royal Canadian Mounted Police put me up at their
barracks and gave me the run of their canteen. It was perfect.
Perfect, that is, except for one thing. There was nothing I could
do. *Super Silver* had been put in bond by the Customs people and
there it had to remain until cleared. That was to take three
days.

It was being kept in a huge shed in the Furness Withy docks

under lock and key. I persuaded the Customs men to unlock the door. They did so and slid it back a few inches until I was able to stick my head inside. The scene before me set all my worries at rest. With great understanding *Silver* had been laid on a matting of old blankets and sacks and covered with huge dust sheets. There was nothing I could have done any better for her. I walked back to my double room with private shower at the Mounties' barracks with a much lighter heart. Those good people at St Johns who have lived side by side with the cruel sea for so many years didn't give me any time to brood.

One of the Mounties drove me up to the old tower on Signal Hill overlooking the entrance to St Johns harbour. It was from here that Marconi transmitted the world's first transatlantic radio message. Another Mountie took me to his home for tea and to meet his wife and kids. And yet another asked me quite solemnly if I would like to go to church.

Never having been much of a churchgoer, his question took me off guard for a few seconds. I gaped at him like a stranded fish. Then suddenly the penny dropped. He was gently asking me if I wanted to pray. In fact I got the distinct impression that he felt anybody planning to row the Atlantic jolly well ought to pray.

At first I made the excuse that as I had not expected to be going anywhere, except to sea, from St Johns, I had not bothered to pack a formal shirt or suit. It was a pretty lame excuse and it sounded like it.

It did not put that Mountie off one bit. Within minutes he had every Mountie in that barrack block searching his kit for spare suits, shirts, shoes and ties. As practically every Mountie in those barracks was about six feet tall on average, it was no easy task to find the gear to fit my five feet six inches.

Finally they found a man just two inches taller than me. I'm fairly bulky in the shoulders, so I filled the jacket quite well, even though it was a bit on the long side. The trousers, however, concertina'd round my ankles. There was no time for alterations—in any case I would be wearing them but once— so we just rolled the trousers up until they were the right length.

I was unlucky with shirts. My neck measures sixteen and a half inches. The Mountie whose suit I borrowed measured just sixteen inches, so one of his shirts was out of the question. We decided that one of the larger ones would just have to do. The neck fitting was not too bad at all, but it covered me almost to my knees and ballooned around me like an air-filled tent. When I was finally kitted out there were a few good-natured grins on the faces of my new friends. 'Gee, Tom,' said one, 'you won't win the title of the year's best-dressed man but you don't have to be a dude to go to church.'

At ten-thirty the next morning (Sunday, 11 May) the man who had originally suggested to his Mountie friend that I might like to go to church turned up at the barracks to drive me to the church in his car. Harold Squires, a civil servant in the St Johns government offices, and his wife Jean treated me like a son. They fed me, cared for me and told me I was free to use their house as if it were my own.

Their superb friendliness while I was waiting for *Super Silver* to be cleared from bond probably did more than anything to stop me worrying and fretting over lost time. Their children, Elizabeth, Robin, Ann, Jean and David, made me feel like some sort of hero. And, above all, they made me feel like a brother.

The next time I did any praying was well out in the Atlantic and the Squires family were included in my prayers. They will always be part of my memories.

On Tuesday morning *Super Silver* was carefully lowered into the icy waters of St Johns harbour. There was a cutting wind and the temperature was near freezing.

For all I cared it could have been thirty degrees below on that wonderful morning. *Super Silver* and I were together again. She bobbed there unloaded and high in the water like a white-painted float. Above her name painted on the forward turtle decking I had painted the winged dagger badge of the SAS, complete with regimental motto: 'Who dares wins'. I was beginning to feel more and more 'at home'.

I set about loading *Silver*. It was quite a job. Fully loaded she would weigh just on one ton. Luckily I found three very willing volunteer helpers down on those docks: three Newfoundland teenagers who wouldn't rest until I allowed them to help me. In that biting wind Glenn and John Allen and Michael Guihan helped as if their very lives depended on it. By late evening *Silver* was almost fully loaded, if somewhat untidily. The arrangement of the stores could be left until the morning, but one thing nagged me. I didn't like to leave her unguarded all night. I was just deciding that then would be as good a time as any to start sleeping on board when the lads asked what I was going to do about guarding *Silver*.

I told them and they wouldn't have it at any price. 'Oh no, Tom,' said Glenn. 'You need to get all the sleep you can. We'll guard the boat.' And they did. One of them hurried off home to get an air pistol, although I must say I hadn't exactly envisaged that an armed guard would be necessary, and Glenn borrowed his father's car.

They drew lots for a system of two-hour watches and one stayed awake while the other two slept in the car. Needless to say, *Silver* passed a completely undisturbed night with such sterling guardians by her side. The boys themselves did not pass such a peaceful night. At dawn a passing Mountie patrol car spotted one of them walking up and down the dockside. Questions were asked and finally the boys managed to convince them they were on guard. I certainly had a lot of friends looking after my interests in St Johns.

The next few days were spent in arranging my stores in such a way that it would ensure *Super Silver* riding just right in the water. I packed and repacked and then repacked that boat again before I was finally satisfied. Her trim was a matter of some concern to passing locals. Gnarled fishermen and deep-sea sailors would look down at her with dubious frowns. Sincere advice came from all sides. 'Her head is too far down in the water, lad.' 'Your seat is not far enough aft.' 'You'll have to shift two or three of your water bags to get rid of that slight list to starboard.'

One man, however, kept a constant seasoned eye on all I was doing. Big Ed Gedden, the paymaster in the Furness Withy office, would come down to the quayside two or three times a day, run a casually expert eye over *Silver* and give his verdict. Finally I had it right even by his stringent standards. 'That's as

right as you'll ever get her, son,' were his words of approval.
'From now on it's up to you.'

Back in his office where every day he gave me tea, and sandwiches made by his wife, Big Ed casually drawled: 'You know
it's going to be hellish cold out there, son. What have you got
to protect your hands? If your hands freeze up, and they'll be
the first to get it, you'll be done.'

I showed him the gloves I had: one pair of leather and one
pair of woollen. 'I'll give it to you straight, son,' he said kindly.
'For all the good they are you might as well be without.'

He explained there was only one article of the glove-maker's
art which could possibly stand up to the weather I would have
to face off the Newfoundland coast.

'The Portuguese dory fishermen who come here every year,'
he said, 'have the right answer. They wear specially oiled wool
mittens which even when soaked never lose their effectiveness.
Just wring them out, slip them back on and they go right on
keeping your hands warm. I'll get you a pair.'

Big Ed was as good as his word. A Portuguese fishing vessel
had pulled into St Johns earlier that week. A short visit to the
skipper and Big Ed was back with the mittens. They lived
up to every word of recommendation he had lavished on
them.

By Saturday morning 17 May the moment of truth had
arrived. The temperature had neither appreciably improved
nor worsened. If anything the wind had slightly dropped. The
sun was shining. The Canadian and US Navy weather reports
repeated the forecast they had made each morning: 'No ap-
preciable movement in the ice-pack which remains in the region
of Bonavista Bay about 120 miles north of St Johns. There are a
few icebergs in the area but these too are well north of St Johns
and show no signs of southerly movement.'

Their reports paralleled those of the weather station at St
Johns Airport. There seemed no doubt about it . . . it was time
to go.

At the invitation of the Squires family I spent the Friday
night at their house. Mrs Squires prepared an enormous dinner
for me which I literally wolfed. Their teenage son David asked
me: 'How do you feel, Tom?' I admitted I was feeling the same

sort of butterflies that had fluttered around my tummy when I made my first parachute jump.

I slept like a top, ate an enormous breakfast of eggs, bacon and toast and drank three huge cups of tea. The Squires were truly sad. With a flask of tea and a large bag of sandwiches—it looked enough to last a month—made by Mrs Squires, we all piled into the car and made for the dockside.

There was quite a crowd to watch me climb down into *Super Silver*. Fishermen, sailors, townsfolk, local TV cameramen and pressmen and the *Sunday Express* had sent Peter Vane to keep an eye on things.

I looked round at the supplies lashed down in position. The only space left was literally where I would sit and place my feet. There was not an inch to spare. Still, I thought, better to have it all now and throw it away later than dump it now and be sorry later.

Somebody threw me a copy of a girlie magazine and shouted: 'There you are, Tom . . . that'll give you something to keep you heading for home.' Suddenly I was aware of all the experienced seamen in that waiting group. They were waiting to see what sort of a job I would make of handling *Super Silver*. None of them had seen me row. The only rowing I had done at St Johns had been late on Friday afternoon when nobody was around. I had taken *Silver* a few yards from one side of the quay to the other to be ready for the off.

I suddenly felt terribly self-conscious. I lay down on top of the supplies as casually as I could and carefully peeled and ate a banana. Maybe it sounds a little flashy, but it helped to calm me down.

I looked at my watch. It was well past 8.30 am. 'Well,' I said to everybody, 'it's no good hanging around. I might as well start now so that at least I'll be out of the harbour before dark.' There was laughter all round at that crack. I stood up and somebody handed me a bottle of whisky. 'There you are, Tom, christen *Super Silver* with that.'

I did just that. Standing forward I poured the entire bottle over *Silver*'s bow. There were a few sad eyes amongst that crowd. I think that is when they decided I was truly mad.

The TV cameramen asked for a few more shots. I reached up

and pumped as many outstretched hands as I could reach, gently refused a request from one old-timer to have his photograph taken in the boat with me, and shouted, much louder than I really intended, 'Let go the mooring lines.'

The ends splashed into the water and I pulled the first stroke of my trip to Ireland. I'll never forget all those watching faces as I rowed for the open sea. Some of them gave me the creeps. I'll swear they thought they were watching the departure of a man who would never see land again.

I shrugged off the shivers and told myself: 'Well, we'll just have to wait and see. One thing for sure . . . I'll find out before they do.'

2 | Sea legs and blisters
17-23 May

It was a long pull through the placid harbour waters. I concentrated on getting to know *Silver* as I bent my back in a not-
too-regular rowing rhythm. My feelings were a tumbled mixture of relief to be under way at last; wondering how I would
fare; hoping the weather would hold good. But one thing I
knew for sure . . . I would walk on land again. I didn't know
when. I was prepared for it to be a long time. But I surely
would.

The faces on the quayside, all turned towards me, became
small pink ovals and then dwindled to tiny white dots. They
had stopped waving and were now silent. The last shout of
'Good luck!' had been called, the last piece of advice given.
There was nothing *they* could do except watch.

I headed for the narrows—the immediate exit from St Johns
harbour to the Atlantic Ocean. On each side of the tight chan-
nel heavy dark brown cliffs lowered themselves to sea-level and
became a huge jumble of jagged rocks. Around them the water
foamed and swirled, breaking each striking wave into angry
clouds of white spray before breaking up and skittering back
as if trying to rejoin the receding swell.

Newfoundland has miles of coastline like that. I had been
warned about it. Old fishermen who had risked their lives for
years around these shores had warned me of what they called
'the draw of the land'—an all-compelling force which tried
to drag you back, to dash you in savage triumph on those
treacherous rocks.

They had told me, oh, so many times: 'Once you're through
those narrows, son, keep pulling. Get away from that coast.
Don't stop rowing until the land is out of sight.' I intended to
do just that.

Still with me was the small flotilla, about eight in all, of
fishing launches which kept company with me into the open

sea. Some were carrying pressmen and TV cameras. Others were carrying the plainly curious. Except for the sound of the chugging engines of their boats they too were silent. 'God,' I groaned, 'they look so bloody gloomy.' I stopped rowing just long enough to give the nearest boat a wave and yell: 'Cheer up, you're not going all the way.'

A raised hand or two in response was the only answer. I discovered months later that it was my rowing style which had been causing the gloom. It had given rise to a certain amount of concern amongst those watchers who were experienced in matters of the sea.

'He's digging his oars too deep.'

'His hands are too close together.'

'Holy cow—he won't clear land by next weekend, not rowing like that.'

I'm only too glad I did not hear those muttered comments. I didn't need anyone to tell me I was a raw novice when it came to handling boats. I had long ago made up my mind that what I didn't know I would just have to learn, on the spot, when it counted most. Believe me, the will to survive is a powerful tutor. In any case, I would rather have sunk like a stone, there and then, than even think of turning back.

Then I was through the narrows and in the open sea at last.

Silver was grabbed by a huge twisting swell. She slewed and rolled in uncontrollable ponderous lurching movements like a bucking bronco trying to unseat its rider in slow motion. Each gunwale dipped in laborious never-stopping arcs as she heeled from side to side. One moment I would be pulling with all my strength with both oars in the water but making no headway at all. *Silver* seemed to stop dead as the incoming swell tipped her bows skyward and tried to slide her backwards into the bottom of the trough from which she had just climbed.

Within seconds the next swell swung her round almost broadside on to the incoming water, leaving me with the impression of trying to row along the side of a hill with one oar jammed in the ground, the other waving aimlessly in the air. I was somewhat stunned by the fact that I didn't seem to be getting much help from the outgoing tide. I had left St Johns on the turn of the tide, intent on dragging every ounce of advantage from it to get me well beyond that rocky coastline. In actual fact I felt as if I was fighting an incoming tide all the way. It seemed a hell of a way to start my grand adventure. I felt quite a clown.

Sweat poured off me as I wrestled to keep *Silver* on as even a course as possible. Before starting I had donned a thick woollen shirt, two sweaters, jeans and a suit of oilskins. Although the sun was bright in a cloudless sky the temperature at St Johns had been 43°F, eleven degrees above freezing. Now I was dripping.

Each lurching movement of the boat had my body, from the haunches up, twisting from side to side and backwards and forwards in a continuous pendulum movement, while the muscles in my legs became rock hard with tension as I braced them against the floorboards.

Just three-quarters of an hour out and already one of my pet schemes to provide myself with a spot of comfort was crumbling. Before leaving I had combed the shops of St Johns to find a wedge-shaped plastic cushion to lash to my thwart. Now I knew it was no good. It had me sitting too high, leaving me with the sensation that I was squatting above the level of the gunwales with a bird's-eye view of the water. The real trouble, however, was that no matter how tightly it was lashed, there was still movement. *Silver* would roll one way, the cushion another and my body yet another. It was no good. It would have to go. I would just have to squat on hard wood all the way.

I stopped rowing long enough to unlash the cushion, throw it into my little shelter and strip off down to shirt and jeans. 'Now,' I told *Silver*, grabbing the oars again, 'let's get down to it.' Gradually things began to go right. The wind, which had been north-east when I set out, swung round to the east, and I became used to the movement of *Silver*. At last I felt as if I belonged to her. I actually felt we were moving. Slow . . . but moving in the right direction. East.

Eight or ten miles out the accompanying boats began turning back to St Johns. One by one they circled me, shouted 'Good luck', and headed for home. I watched as they rolled off in the swell. As they slid into each trough they disappeared from sight until the next swell carried them into vision again like some huge conjuring trick. As they bobbed up and down I realised I must be presenting exactly the same picture to them.

Within a short time there was but one boat left. Bob Ivery, the St Johns carpenter who did so much to help me put the final touches to *Silver*'s woodwork, was alone in his launch. He stayed with me for about another hour. Then he too turned for home. It was a full five minutes before I realised I had stopped rowing to watch him. I shook myself and got on with what I was out there to do . . . row.

Alone at last? Not quite. About half an hour later a frigate of the Royal Canadian Navy steamed past me about a hundred yards off my port side. They knew what I was doing there. The lads lined the rails to wave and the wind carried the tail end of their shouts to me, but I could not make out what they were saying. Then, with a breezy toot-toot-toot on her siren, she headed north on ice patrol.

I rowed until four o'clock in the afternoon. I could still see what I thought was the outline of the land, but I figured I was far enough now to be reasonably safe. I poured tea from the flask Mrs Squires had given me and munched steadily through the great pile of sandwiches she had made. I was happy to find that my appetite had not been affected in any way at all. I had thought I might be sick. But luckily there had not been the slightest sign of queasiness.

I sipped the tea, stared out at the fading daylight and took stock of the situation. The sea was roughening. *Silver* was beginning to be thrown about a bit and the temperature had dropped to 40°F. The wind had swung round yet again and was driving me south. I decided the best thing to do was put out the sea anchor and get my head down.

It was five o'clock in the morning before I opened my eyes again. And I was sick. I had thought it would overtake me but I didn't know whether it was seasickness or just a result of the build-up of excitement of the last couple of days. I just draped myself over *Silver*'s side and hung there until I felt empty. Finally I lifted my head and, through streaming eyes, stared across the sea. Something seemed to be missing and, at first, I couldn't understand what it was. Then light dawned. The land was completely out of sight.

That bout of sickness was only the beginning of the alarming initiation ceremony to the discomforts of the Atlantic. Across the palms of my hands spread a slight prickling feeling. As the day passed by, each stroke of the oar seared into my hands as if the skin was wearing paper thin. Then the blisters began to balloon. There were three on the palm of each hand. I could feel them growing larger as I rowed. By midday they were so swollen the handles of the oars felt as if they had doubled in thickness. I could hardly clasp my fingers round them.

Immediate and rough treatment was the only answer. I bit through each blister in turn, carefully nicking a hole as near the middle as possible, with the corners of my eye teeth, then squeezed out as much water as I could. Then I plunged my hands in and out of a bucket of sea water several times to try to pickle the dead skin into some state of firmness in order to protect the patches of raw flesh underneath. They stung like blazes but at least the oars felt normal size once more.

All this had taken some time and I had, of course, had to take off my Portuguese mittens. A 30 mph wind slicing down from the north west had been eating into my bare hands. And the sea water had not helped. It was cold, bitterly and numbingly cold. The wind had been travelling across several hundreds of miles of Arctic ice and, by the time it hit me, was in a highly refrigerated state. And the weather was getting even colder.

On Monday morning, 19 May, I woke just after dawn to below-freezing temperatures and found *Silver* covered from stem to stern with a layer of thick frost. I sat up with the sleeping bag tucked tightly up to my chin and, pulling aside the canvas front of my little shelter, looked round *Silver* as she glistened in the dull morning light. It was like sitting in the middle of a birthday cake.

A slight fog was hanging around and I wondered where I could be. I had not yet bothered to fix a position and I decided to let it slide for another day or two. My compass told me I was heading east as near as damn it and that was all that mattered at that stage.

I sat there for quite a while with *Silver* rocking gently in a 10 mph breeze. I have never enjoyed getting up on cold morn-

c

ings. In the distance to the north of *Silver* I spotted a couple of whales, but either they did not see me or considered me unworthy of their attention, for they kept going on their chosen course until they vanished from sight.

It was a lonely day. I saw no ships, no birds, no planes. There was, however, one incongruous homely touch. A child's plastic potty came drifting past. It was bright yellow and I watched it as it bobbed away into the distance. There was no doubt that out in the Atlantic one's attention is caught by the slightest object as if it were the big event of the day. As I rowed I found myself thinking of that yellow pot. Where could it have come from? How old was the child? A boy or a girl? What sort of a home was he or she growing up in?

My thoughts switched to my foster parents on their farm near Aylesbury. John Venn and his wife had taken me in from the orphanage, Fegan's Homes at Stony Stratford, when I was fourteen. The Venns and their farm were the only real home I had ever known. They had been a wonderful couple to me and I had revelled in the open-air life of the farm. I knew that back there it would be a marvellous time of the year. John would be getting ready for the mowing. I could almost smell the sweetness of fresh-cut grass. The farm stayed in my thoughts for most of the day. I crawled into my shelter that night thinking: 'With luck it'll be harvest time when I get back.'

But there was to be little sleep ahead for me. The strongest winds I had yet experienced began building up through the night. The wind whipped through the locking holes in the telescopic radio aerial whistling like a demented steam kettle continuously on the boil. The most I managed was an extremely erratic session of cat-naps. For the first time I felt *Silver* being really knocked about. The sea thudded into her, shaking her so much that the vibrations did not have time to fade away before the next lot of water attacked. She spun, bounced and rocked.

That corny old joke about 'forgetting to shake the bottle before taking the medicine' struck me as rather suitable. Waves were breaking over *Silver* every fifteen to twenty minutes. Huge waves, each one, I reckon, loading flimsy little *Silver* with somewhere near forty gallons of water.

The rest of the night was a living nightmare. It was pitch

black relieved occasionally only by the slight illumination afforded by the swirling phosphorous shining a ghost-like green on the water. That was the only means I had of visually checking the level of water inside *Silver* and deciding when to pump. I completely lost count of the number of times I crawled out of my shelter to go to work on those pumps. Finally I just knelt on my bundled-up sleeping bag in the shelter entrance holding the pump handles and ready to pump at a moment's notice. Never has a night seemed so long. I propped myself up, my chest heaved with the effort of pumping. The blood tingling as it raced through my arms, and my overheated body feeling as if it was steaming against the bitter night air.

Hours, days, later, or so it seemed, there was a faint grey light around me. Walls of waves, topped with white fury, racing towards me became distinctly visible against the sky. Dawn had arrived and with it I was able to see exactly what was happening. It was a toss-up whether or not I would have welcomed a freak of nature which would have plunged me back beneath the cover of the pitch-black night. This was my first sight, my first taste, of the Atlantic's favourite sport—playing pat-ball with the smallest boat it could find.

I have been a physical person all my life, relying mainly on my strength and will-power to cope with whatever situation came my way. But this was something I had no experience of whatsoever. Never have I felt quite so utterly helpless. *Silver* was in the grip of winds of at least 50 mph and there was absolutely nothing I could do . . . except pump for my life. Forty-foot-high waves rolled towards me, under me, over me and past me in a never-ending avalanche. Awesome, unnerving, frightening . . . it was all of that. Yet the strangest feeling was that of being hypnotised by this fantastic show of nature's power.

I wasn't exactly frightened, but I reckon I would have become well and truly scared if I had sat there too long just looking at the sea. The extraordinary thing was the difficulty I had in forcing myself not to look. Those heaving, rushing waters dragged at my eyes like a magnet.

Foolishly I decided that if I tried rowing for a bit my mind would be too fully occupied to worry about the sea and I would find welcome relief in physical effort. For nearly half an hour I engaged myself in this futile and frantically unequal contest. Twice, probably the only times the oars really entered the water, I was within an ace of having the oars snatched from my grasp. I became obsessed with the idea that to lose one oar would be a disgrace, but to lose both . . . that would stamp me as an idiot. I shipped the oars and lashed them down as tightly as I could. I imagine a more experienced seafarer would never have bothered in the first place. He would wisely have conserved his energy rather than spend it in such a useless manner.

For the first time I began to realise what was meant by the term seamanship. Yet, I wondered, what more could the best sailor in the world have done? The answer would surely be nothing more than wedge himself in the bottom of *Silver* and hope for the best. I was beginning to learn.

Silver was now running before the wind. She was fairly zipping along and, with a following wind, was not taking nearly so much water inboard. But it was a wind from the north, driving me hard to the south and far off my eastward course. I cursed this unfriendly wind. 'If you have to blow . . . blow me east,' I yelled it into the storm as I watched the compass needle quivering relentlessly towards the south.

I bitterly resented every yard off my course, more bitterly than a Shylock grudging every fraction of a lost copper. For every yard would have to be regained, fought for and bought back. And the price I would have to pay would be time, invaluable time. Every yard was a knife-thrust to my ambition to be the first man to row the Atlantic single-handed. Every yard was a bonus to John Fairfax somewhere far to the south of me.

Suddenly I realised I was shivering. I had not eaten for nearly twenty-four hours. I knew no matter how difficult it proved I would have to get some hot food inside me soon. While constant pumping had been necessary the cold had gone unnoticed. Now I felt ice-blue all over. There was absolutely no way of keeping dry. I was damp right through to the skin and there was nothing I could do about it except grin and bear it.

A mug of tea first would put new life into me. Propped up on one elbow in the bottom of *Silver*, and with the wind snuffing out match after match, it took nearly fifteen minutes to get my camping cooker going. But the kettle finally boiled. I took off my mittens and wrapped my hands round the steaming mug and gulped at the thick dark brew, almost syrupy with sugar and condensed milk. But cooking a meal was out of the question right then. I settled for dry biscuits and curry paste spooned from the jar. It really was a delicious meal.

Then I crawled into my shelter to nibble a piece of chocolate while I lay there looking up at a photograph I had pinned to the ceiling of the shelter. It was of the man who had been my hero ever since, quite by accident, I read a book about his adventures during my early Army days. Antarctic explorer Sir Ernest Shackleton captured my imagination as nobody had ever done before. His refusal to give up, no matter how hard the going, his tremendous capabilities, his leadership and his tremendous strength of character, not only inspired me but altered my whole way of life. Privately, to me, he was the Boss.

I looked up at the salt-flecked photograph, wondering: 'How long will I be out here?' The Boss had been in the Antarctic for eighteen months, so my stint was nothing more than a week-end by comparison. My mind drifted back over the years. Alone out here I was beginning to think more and more of my past life. Isolation is a marvellous state for being able to sort things out into some perspective.

When I had left the orphanage to join the Venns at their farm I had just turned fourteen. Ten months later, at the age of fifteen, I got the wanderlust. I left the farm, found digs at Uckfield in Sussex and got myself a job as a hod-carrier on a building site. With a few quid in my pocket each week I felt I was grown up . . . a man. In actual fact I was nothing more than a cocksure kid. The Venns had been kindness itself and had given me the nearest thing to a home and family I am ever likely to know. But I didn't appreciate it in those days. I wanted to be on my own . . . to do exactly as I liked.

The net result was that I fell into bad company and became a bit of a Teddy Boy. Although I always had a job and, even then, saved as much cash as I could, I indulged in a spot of lead-stealing from church roofs. I made a few bob, of course, but it was not the money. I found it exciting. My pursuit of

thrills once landed me in Bow Street court. With an equally
rebellious chum I had gone to London for a few days. We spent
most of the time stealing motor bikes and seeing how far we
could travel before they ran out of petrol. We were caught and
I was bound over for a year. That didn't bother me at the time.
I was still my own boss, and riding high, wide and handsome.
The thought that I was leading an utterly useless life never
entered my empty head.

Then came a chance meeting with an old friend from the
boys' home. He was in the uniform of a British paratrooper.
For no other reason than the fact he was in the Army, I joined
the Parachute Regiment straight away. I was the ripe age of
seventeen and a half.

I chuckled as my mind raced back over the years, for I had
taken to the Army like a duck to water. One thing was certain.
If I had not joined up I would not be out here in the most
expensive personal possession I had ever owned . . . *Super Silver*.
I knew I was where I belonged at last. Neither the storm nor
the fact that I was still being blown off course bothered me
right then. I was beginning to enjoy the Atlantic.

Feeling I could tackle anything now, I tried the radio for the
first time. I picked up the station at St Johns. They were playing a disc of Mary Hopkin singing *Goodbye*.

'Not yet, little lady,' I muttered. 'Not goodbye by a long
chalk.'

The song made me feel a little nostalgic and sentimental
about all the good friends who had helped me. It seemed impossible to believe that less than four days ago I had been sitting
in the Squires home back in St Johns, signing autographs which
the children had demanded. Suddenly I realised the radio
newscaster was talking of the US moon shot. They were expected to land the following day. I hoped everything would go
smoothly for them and hoped for a good tomorrow for myself.

But it was another sleepless night by the pumps, with the
morning ushering in even stronger winds. They were buffeting
Silver at a rate of between sixty to seventy miles an hour. I
blessed the sturdy craftsmanship of those Yorkshire boatbuilders
who had constructed *Silver*. Flimsy she may look, but flimsy she
most certainly was not when it came to standing up to the

Atlantic. I am sure that *Silver*'s superb performance under such stern conditions helped to build my self-confidence. It was also creating a relationship between man and boat which was to grow into an unbreakable bond. In the old days, they say, ships were made of wood and men of iron. If I was not to fail *Silver* I would have to try to give a twentieth-century twist to that old legend.

It was to be yet another day of pumping, with little chance of snatching even a short doze. Lack of sleep in itself is no real hardship. After three years in the paratroops and three years in the Special Air Service roughing it comes as second nature. I was grateful for my Army training, especially that in the SAS. It is probably the most rigorously trained Army unit in the world today. Trained to fight on his own, to live on his own and to survive on his own, each man becomes what must be the most physically self-reliant human package known to any walk of life today. And part of the secret is knowing, and believing, you can cope with practically anything and everything.

Luck, however, does have a part to play as in most things. Because of the cold and the water I had muffled myself up in two thick woolly undervests, a thick flannel shirt, a pullover, a seaman's heavy roll-collar sweater and two sets of waterproof clothing. A bit cumbersome, to say the least, but they turned out to be a godsend. During the turmoil of the past two days and nights I had been flung about the tiny open space which made up the cockpit of *Silver*. I had been thudded into the gunwales, the cooker, the edge of the shelter roof and the compass itself, which jutted out from the roof like a knobbly-headed battering ram. By rights I should have been black and blue from head to toe. Thanks to the mass of clothing, I had been cushioned against the most severe effects of such a battering and merely felt a little sore.

Here was another lesson learned in double-quick time. There was no sense in trying to stand up or move about too much while *Silver* was bucketing about. I had tried to stand, to move about as much as possible simply to give myself the sense of doing something. Rowing had been out of the question for hours. And for hours I lay on my side, half in and half out of the shelter. My back was wedged against the pack that was my RAF inflatable dinghy and my feet jammed tight against the supplies which filled up the rest of *Silver*. During the morning I had managed to cook up some of my dehydrated curry and had left some in the pressure cooker ready to eat, hot or cold, for I had no idea when this damnable storm would ease off long enough for me to prepare a reasonable meal.

Lying there, wedged in, while *Silver* lurched, rolled, rocked and trembled, I became very conscious of my utter helplessness to do anything constructive. It was not a mood of despair. It was a feeling of complete frustration which swept over me. The only thing to do was to take stock of the situation which faced me if the storm continued for much longer. First the water which was continuing to come inboard. The main comforter was that not nearly so much was breaking over me as during the first few hours. I had, however, become fully aware of the Atlantic's ferocious talent for sudden change. A shift of wind, a breaking roller and *Silver* could be swamped. I had by this time become fully confident of the efficiency of the pumps. They had been working splendidly.

By my rough calculations they were capable of shifting about twenty gallons of water a minute. So far that had been generously adequate. One huge doubt nagged at my mind. What if *Silver* took such a ducking that she filled up beyond the emptying rate of which the pumps were capable? There was only one way of attempting to cope with such a situation.

My five-gallon baling bucket, lashed at the back of the seat, would have to be brought into use. I reckoned that I would be able to shift about sixty gallons a minute with that. But two questions remained unanswered:

1. How long could I maintain such back-breaking pace? Not very long.

2. What if the flooding of *Silver* was so great that not even sixty gallons a minute could cope? I shrugged and decided to wait until it happened.

Just before twilight I managed to get my stove lit after ten minutes of effort and the use of nearly half a box of matches. I managed to keep the matches reasonably dry by wrapping them in two bags of heavy-duty polythene and buttoning them down in the breast pocket of my shirt beneath the outer covering of sweaters and oilskins.

The left-over curry came quickly to the boil in the pressure cooker. There were just ten spoonfuls, but they were every bit as good as a full-scale banquet. There is no doubt that regular hot food and drink is vital. Without it I feared I could become a victim of exposure and even more helpless—although that didn't seem possible—than ever. It was just another problem to add to my mental preoccupations which saved me from worrying too much about my enforced inactivity and the bitter realisation that I was still drifting towards the south.

But the screaming wind stayed with me right through another night. By this time I was not bothering to creep into my sleeping bag in case I had to move in a hurry. It left me free to grab the pumps within split seconds. I just wrapped my Army rubberised poncho around me and cat-napped in between the pumping, the never-ending pumping sessions.

I suddenly realised that the blisters on my hands must be hardening up or else I had become so used to them I did not feel them any longer. When I grabbed the pump handles I no longer felt the burning sensation slashing straight across the palms. It was small enough consolation, but to me it seemed like the boon of a lifetime. Hardly, however, had I congratulated myself on that spot of luck when I realised I had more serious troubles to deal with. With the morning the Arctic winds had still come rushing in from the north.

I had been aware for the past twenty-four hours of peculiar twinges of pain in my feet. As the time passed, the twinges became more severe. But they had lasted no more than a few seconds and, in any case, I had too much to think about. But now they were giving real trouble. They ached constantly with a dull, nagging pain. I could sense they were swollen so much that my sea-boots felt drum-tight. The cold, I told myself, is getting at them. Soon, very soon, I knew, I would have to take off my boots and do something about my feet. Perhaps I would have tended to them there and then—and saved myself a lot of misery—if the wind had not, at long last, shown signs of dropping.

'I can't waste time on my feet now,' I told myself. 'Any

minute I shall be able to row again.' At that moment rowing was the most important thing in the whole world. War could have broken out somewhere, they could have been running pleasure trips to the moon or an unknown relative could have left me £1,000,000 and I would have turned my back on it all for the greatest privilege open to me—conditions which would allow me to row.

The McClean luck held good. By about 2 pm the storm died away and the winds became a whisper at a mere fifteen miles per hour. I would row now if I never rowed again. I was grinning all over my face as my fingers scrabbled away at the sea-soaked lashings holding the oars along *Silver*'s gunwales. Then the blades were in the water and I was bending my back. I was truly happy for the first time in two and a half days. Except for a lunch break of really piping hot curry and a couple of tea breaks, I rowed right through that wonderful day, through the evening, past twilight and into the night. I did not ship the oars until 9 pm.

And I felt great . . . absolutely on top of the world. What did it matter that I had had to row south as the wind was still from the north? What did it matter that I had not seen the sun since the first day out? What did it matter that I had not seen a single ship apart from the Canadian frigate on that first day? I felt that I would not give a damn if I did not see either the sun or a ship until I got home.

It was only a matter of time. I recalled what John Ridgway had said during that chat so many months before. 'Don't forget, Tom, weakness or strength, whatever happens, it is all in the mind.' That is for sure. I had enough food and water to last more than four months. I had found my sea legs. I didn't care how long it took to get home. I just knew, beyond all possible doubt, that I would get home.

Like the Atlantic itself, my moods were capable of radical change within seconds. Although one never loses sight of the main objective, never lets go of the long-term plan, there are times when one just lives for the brief moment of elation or depression. Nothing else at all seems to matter. My spirits were soaring as I crawled into my shelter. I snuggled down into my sleeping bag and dropped off like a log. I don't know what time it was when I woke. I have no idea of what disturbed my sleep. But automatically I lifted the side of the shelter's canvas cover for a precautionary look around.

Away on the starboard side I spotted a light flashing on and off. Those high spirits of mine dropped like a stone. My immediate fear was that I had drifted back towards the land and that flashing signal was the warning of a lightship. Scrambling to my feet, I leaned on the starboard gunwale and stared hard and long, almost without blinking, at that depressing light. Sheer, blessed relief flooded through me as I realised I was looking at the lights of a ship. The flashing effect was caused by the movement of the waves momentarily cutting it off from my sight every few seconds or so.

I was not destined to sleep peacefully that night. I was roused later by a sound I could not make out at all. With eyes wide open in the dark I lay there trying to figure it out. With a start I realised it sounded for all the world like the heavy breathing of a large animal. For one stupid moment I imagined a sea serpent coiled up on the roof of my shelter. 'Oh nuts!' I told myself. Nevertheless I kept dead still and listening hard. Finally I crept out to investigate.

The explanation was so simple I had to burst out laughing. The rudder ropes which stretched across the shelter and down to cleats on each gunwale had worked a little loose. Although the movement this allowed the rudder was extremely slight, it was, nevertheless, enough to set those ropes rubbing with regular persistence across the shelter roof. I tightened the ropes and took my third stab at sleep.

I slept till dawn and woke feeling fresh and anxious to row. I made tea and wolfed a tin of sardines for breakfast. The tea was more than welcome. For this was the coldest day yet. The temperature was at freezing point and snow was thickly falling. It was not, however, settling on *Silver*. It reminded me of the pack-ice lying just over a hundred miles to the north. I estimated that a sudden storm, such as I had been through, with southerly winds could place me in the ice and that would be the end of me and *Silver*.

I was grateful that the winds had dropped, but they were still against me. The day began with a 15 mph south-easterly which slowly edged round until it was due east. I was being blown back to Newfoundland and it was no use trying to row. The sea anchor was out all day in a bid to stem that drift back to the land. Luckily the east wind soon dropped to just 5 mph.

Luckily? I'd had a lot of luck already. Could I ask for more? I was sure I had got the hang of things out there. In just three days I'd learned more about survival in the Atlantic than I would ever have picked up in a year of practice rowing. One of the arts of survival, however, is cheek . . . the cheek to look for, and expect, far more than one deserves. And tomorrow I would be looking for a steady west wind. That would be real luck. All the luck I needed for now, at least.

3 | In deep freeze
24-27 May

When planning this trip I had meticulously studied the currents and prevalent winds of the North Atlantic Ocean. On paper it had, to me, seemed comparatively straightforward. Broadly speaking, the Admiralty charts showed that my northern route was largely covered by predominant westerly winds and the westward-flowing Gulf Stream. That stream, carrying life-giving warmth from the Gulf of Florida to the shores of Britain, was the master key to my plan. Once in that, I thought, and I would be getting some help from the sea instead of having to fight it all the way.

There were, however, two calculated risks which I had to weigh carefully before making up my mind. Firstly, the iceberg zone spreading well to the south of Newfoundland in May was a hazard instantly challenging, constantly worrisome. The threat of those glacial monsters and how the slightest bump could strip the bottom out of *Silver* was not one I could lightly dismiss. At night it would be like a ghoulish game of Russian roulette. Miss one, miss two . . . but how long could one go on missing and for how many nights? A collision while I was asleep and that would be the end of the adventure before it had really begun.

Secondly, I could expect, with practically 100 per cent certainty, raging gales which could last for days and nights without let-up. Winds of anything between 40 and 70 mph, perhaps more, sweep this area on more than ten days a month. What if my sailing date coincided with those wind-torn days? Would I, with my inexperience, be able to handle *Silver* under such circumstances before I had a chance to become accustomed to the temper of the sea? Yet I considered both risks well worth taking for the benefit I would gain by taking the somewhat shorter route between Newfoundland and the British Isles.

The first gamble paid off handsomely. I did not see a single iceberg. But the winds? That was another matter. They blew as predicted all right . . . but in the wrong direction.

In my opinion the really big obstacle I had to face was the Labrador Current, sometimes known as the Arctic Current. This stream of icy water flows south along the coasts of Labrador and Newfoundland. Originating in Baffin Bay and the west coast of Greenland, it often carries icebergs as far south as the Grand Banks, the submerged plateau which extends 500 miles into the Atlantic Ocean from the southern tip of Newfoundland.

Could I stand the intense cold of that 200-mile-wide icy strip? Would I be able to row strongly enough to offset the southward drag of the current? I figured the answer to both questions was 'Yes'. I also calculated that it would take me roughly two weeks to fight off the clutch of the Labrador Current and slip into the Gulf Stream.

By Saturday, 24 May, I was not nearly so sure. I awoke on the morning of my eighth day out with this problem eating into my brain. I had been blown well off course and, although light, the wind was still from the east. I knew I had been steadily heading south for the last five days. But I had absolutely no way of telling how much vital milage I had made—perhaps lost would be a more appropriate word—to the east. I had made no attempt to plot my position. My only guide was the compass needle remorselessly showing my southward course.

The temptation to start rowing in a bid to swing *Silver* in the right direction just for the satisfaction of seeing that tantalising needle pointing east was almost too great to bear. Three times I unlashed the oars. And three times I lashed them back into place without even dipping them into the water. The realisation that I would lose more ground by trying to row than by just sitting it out won me round to the common-sense point of view.

Four days without a single stroke being pulled stretched into six. Throughout Saturday and Sunday, in temperatures averaging no more than 35°F, I allowed the Atlantic to take *Silver* and me wherever it willed.

Try as I would I could not draw much comfort from the thought that I was being sensible. The continual dull weather of the past seven days showed no signs of lifting. Cheerless clouds and grey seas had become a depressing sight. For the first time, I suppose, the immensity of the water around me began to strike home. I shuddered at the idea of being a professional sailor. But the thought of those thousands of men who earn a living from the sea roused my admiration for them.

Strange that I had never thought of them like this before. Sailors had been . . . well, just sailors. There must be many, far too many, people whose main idea of a sailor conjures up a figure with rolling gait; a happy-go-lucky man whose main preoccupations are getting drunk and plunging into shore brawls; an irresponsible fool who throws his money away on women and gambling. All I can say is if any sailor wants to live that way . . . good luck to him. But I do not think many do choose that as a permanent way of life.

Do they ever think of what lies beneath their ships? I wondered. I tapped the floorboards of *Silver* and thought of the flimsy wooden planking that was all that lay between me and the dark icy depths beneath. The memory of a passage from one of C. S. Forester's books, *The Good Shepherd*, suddenly crowded into my mind:

'And the big ships, to insignificant man so huge and so solid, sank to the sea bottom, to the immemorial ooze in the darkness and cold, with no more ado or stir than would be caused comparatively by specks of dust falling on a ballroom floor.'

If ever disaster struck *Silver* I would be the only candidate for the 'immemorial ooze'. *Silver*'s wooden hull might break into a hundred pieces, but sink they would not. Perhaps the sea would be kind enough to wash those remains on to a tropical beach. In a ridiculous moment of bravado I told myself: 'Even if I have to hold *Silver* together with my bare hands I'll keep going to the end or bust.' An extravagant boast, perhaps. It really boiled down to a vow never to give up.

'Crikey,' I thought, 'I'm getting morbid.' It was a condition of mind which had to be broken. The enforced inactivity had allowed my body to get thoroughly chilled. 'And your brain!' I told myself. I became conscious of the fact that despite sweaters and oilskins I was literally shivering. My clothing had been continually damp for days. And the dampness had penetrated right through to my skin. Now it felt as if I was encased in a skintight suit of ice. As I breathed I watched my breath hang in misty clouds for a fraction of a second before being snatched by that frustrating north-easterly wind.

Like an overworked housewife who relieves the tensions of her day with a cup of tea, I got my cooker going, filled the kettle and huddled round the gas jets. I gulped down two pints of scalding tea before I began to thaw out a little. It is impossible to tell just how much warmth I drew from the gas jets of my cooker. But psychologically they were a perfect tonic. The mere sight of those flickering bluish-yellow flames gave me the same feeling of well-being that one gets from a log fire at Christmas. I did not want to turn that cooker off. Although it was only eleven in the morning, I decided on an early lunch. I boiled up a block of Army dehydrated curry and took as long as I possibly could. To make it last and to make every mouthful as hot as possible I kept the cooker simmering and ate my meal from the pot without once taking it off the flame. Out there, in the words of Henry VIII, 'Manners are a thing of the past'.

There was a certain amount of dreary satisfaction in knowing that I had been right in thinking the Labrador Current would be my biggest obstacle. I was in its grip with a vengeance. An extraordinary feeling of being trapped in a cage of liquid ice ran through me. I had to find a way to beat it. But how? How? How?

I hammered myself with the same question. The answer was always the same. There was nothing to do but stick it out until that damned eternal north-easterly blew itself out. Then perhaps I would be able to get a move on towards that almost mythical Gulf Stream which by now had developed into the only thing that mattered in my life.

Mentally I prodded myself into action. The effects of the tea and the curry would soon wear off. Burning the cooker continuously was out of the question. At all costs I must conserve my supply of gas cylinders. Although I planned on making the journey in a hundred days at most I must try to look ahead. Foreseeing emergencies is part of the art of survival. There was no way of telling exactly how long I would be out here. And if

I overran those hundred days by any length of time I would still have to eat and I would still need hot food. The risk of wasting my gas just could not be taken. Within an hour the knife-thrust of the Labrador air would be needling through to my bones yet again. I had to fight it before I became a quivering jelly with no more thought than to lie down and bury myself as deep as possible in my sleeping bag.

Sitting on the seat, I flapped my arms across my body hard and fast for one or two minutes. Then, with hands on hips, I went through a series of trunk bending and rolling gyrations from my sitting position. I alternated these two exercises with two-minute sessions of basic arms forward and outward stretching. Everything was carried through with as much speed and energy as possible. And throughout it all I would hold my breath until my eyes bulged in my head, then suck in more air and hold my breath again. I kept it up until I could feel the blood rushing through me like a mini Niagara Falls. I did not stop until I was panting and sucking in air like a man who had just run a mile at full tilt all the way.

I had planned to exercise myself in this way, at a more leisurely pace of course, simply to keep fit. I had not counted on it as a means of climbing out of the deep freeze I now found myself in. With heaving chest I crawled into my sleeping bag in a bid to preserve my new sense of warmth as long as possible. As there was nothing I could do until I felt the next attack of warning chills, I tuned the radio to St Johns. I waited for the news broadcast. My name was mentioned and I had the strange experience of listening to someone I did not know saying that I had been at sea for a week.

'Nobody,' the voice said, 'has reported seeing Atlantic rower McClean since he left St Johns on 17 May. And nobody has heard from him. The coastguards have been maintaining a daily radio watch but have heard nothing.'

The thought that a watch was being kept for me was comforting. I dickered with the idea of having a go at getting a radio message through to the land. But it would have meant unlashing the watertight box containing the radio. A simple enough job. Yet I decided against it. I was determined to stick to my original intention of not using the radio for anything

D

except emergencies. I was intent on making the crossing without help; without stopping; without asking passing ships for a single thing except, perhaps, a check on my position.

I am a fairly gabby sort of person by nature. A good natter is something I truly enjoy. Very early in my Army career I had been nicknamed 'Moby' by my pals because, they said, I 'spouted like a whale'. For anything up to a hundred days and more I would be alone. Nobody to talk to; nobody to get fed up with my gossip. There was more than a little doubt in my mind that if I once got into contact with somebody by radio I would be tempted to try it again and again just for the sake of a chat. That did not fit in with my idea of a single-handed Atlantic row.

As for stopping? Well, there were no islands anywhere on my route which might lure me in with visions of hot baths, comfortable beds and fresh food. So I wouldn't be able to stop even if I wanted to do so. And I had not seen a single ship, apart from the Canadian frigate on the first day. Maybe it was rowing the Atlantic the hard way. But I figured if I was going to do it at all that is the way it would have to be. Having braced up my spirits with this re-declaration of my plans, I settled down to waiting out the icy hours which lay ahead.

By this time I was aware that I had a pretty regular case of the snuffles. My nose was running and my eyes were watering. This was no time to go down with 'flu. Popping the kettle on, I dug out my medicine chest. This was a plastic food container with a self-sealing lid which was packed with codeine tablets, glucose tablets, morphine tablets, antiseptic creams, Vaseline, bandages and surgical kit. Nearly half filling a pint mug with neat blackcurrant cordial, I topped it up with boiling water and washed down four codeine tablets as fast as I could. It seemed to work. By the next morning there was hardly a sniff left in me.

Long before the next morning, however, I had to come to grips with yet another problem. I had begun to show the first signs of exposure. My face was raw with the cold. Every time I blew my nose it felt as if I had grabbed an open wound. It was tender, swollen and peeling. Too sore to even blow before long.

Having stowed away my medicine chest and lashed it back

into position I did not want to bother getting it out again. Wedged in a corner by the cooker was an opened sardine tin with a couple of fish which I had been keeping for my tea. The oil was frozen almost solid but I managed to thaw it out a little by holding the tin close to a steaming kettle. I dipped a finger in the oil and gently smeared it over my face and nose, rubbing the remainder into my hands which were also red and swollen.

The stench of sardines must have been pretty powerful but it did not worry me. My nose was so swollen and sore I couldn't smell a thing. The oil was both soothing and warming. I reckoned if I didn't get out of Labrador's grip before long I would have to mask my face as much as possible to shield it against this bitter, cutting temperature and wind.

I decided I would wind a towel around my head, thus covering the exposed forehead, and wrap a scarf found the lower half of my face, covering it to just below the eyes. But first I would apply a thick coating of Vaseline. While working this plan out it suddenly struck me that my water bags had not frozen. These plastic containers, each carrying two gallons of drinking water, had showed no signs of being affected by the weather.

It was impossible to check them all. Most of them were stowed away beneath the floorboards, acting as ballast until needed. It would have meant shifting a lot of the supplies to get at them and then would come the business of re-stowing and lashing everything down again. I couldn't take that chance. In the few days I had been out I had used practically nothing of *Silver*'s stores. It had taken enough trouble to get them arranged so that *Silver*'s trim was just right. To alter that delicate balance now could well be fatal. Too much weight at the head or at the stern, a slight list to either side and the next storm could well capsize *Silver*. I decided that even if they did freeze I would just have to rip them open and chip off pieces of ice small enough to slip into the kettle.

So far the wind had been driving me south and was still doing so. Eternally south. But at least, if that kept up, I *must* eventually end up in warmer waters. Perhaps it would not be where I wanted, but it would be preferable to being blown north.

Counting that small, if frustrating, blessing I felt a little

better, a little more human. In the meantime, however, I had
to get on with the task of preventing myself from freezing solid.
I ran through my exercises for a few minutes once again. This
time, after my body had warmed up, I rose to my feet and,
without thinking, started to stamp them slowly and deliberately. Agonising stabs of pain which ran through my feet from
the toes to just above the ankles reminded me that I still had a
problem which, psychologically, I had been refusing to face.

Gingerly lowering myself on to my sleeping bag, I lifted both
feet in the air. Right then it seemed as if I could not allow them
to be in contact with anything. The dull, slow throbbing had
the effect of shaking my body from head to toe. I held my legs
high as long as I could, then slid towards the bows until I could
rest the backs of my thighs on the edge of my rowing seat,
leaving my feet still levered in mid-air.

I thought the throbbing would never stop. Each pulsating
beat seemed to blow up my feet to such a size I felt sure they
would burst my rubber sea-boots. Gradually, it seemed like
hours, the throbbing died away, leaving a dull ache. This too
gradually faded until once again my feet were so numb that
they might just as well have dropped off for all the feeling that
was left in them.

The danger signals were loud and clear. The problem was
should I treat them now or could I hang on a little longer. I
desperately wanted to hang on as long as I could. For if the
wind changed in my favour I would have to be ready to row,
and row like blazes, in a bid to scramble out of this ice-box. To
be caught with my pants down, or rather with my boots off,
would waste valuable time.

How long would they take to get off? Maybe I would have
to cut them off? No matter what I did to protect them, could
I stand the pressure which would be applied once I started
rowing without the thick rubber soles of my boots to offer what
little shield they could?

The questions drummed through my brain time and time
again and all without an adequate answer. The most important
question was: while still in these freezing temperatures, did the
boots actually offer more protection than anything I could
devise by wrapping my feet in socks, jerseys, towels or anything

else I had in the boat? I finally plumped for keeping them on. I knew I could hold out for a little longer. I had to.

That Sunday, 25 May, become one of the longest days in my life. Frantically seeking ways of keeping myself occupied, and warm, I made a brew and burrowed into my kitbag for a box of letters Paul Sargent had sent to me at St Johns. The instructions in the accompanying note had been explicit. I was to open one each Sunday. They turned out to be letters written by chums back at the SAS headquarters and friends. Paul's idea had been to break the loneliness of the row with a weekly reminder that quite a few people were thinking of me.

The first letter was from Paul himself. He told me not to get tight on the rum—I had some bottles of Navy Neaters on board —as I could still be 'done' for being drunk in charge of a rowing boat. As a matter of fact, I had not touched a drop. That rum was for emergencies or to celebrate seeing a boat. I certainly had nothing to celebrate, and I refused to regard my feet as an emergency. It was ridiculous. If I started tippling at every little set-back I wouldn't have anything for the time I hit real trouble. After all, any amount of emergencies could be ahead of me. I had been out only one week . . . one week? A hundred weeks? What was the difference?

I found myself drifting into temptation as steadily as *Silver* was drifting south. The thought of a shot of that rum was tantalisingly urgent. I thought of the bite of the spirit as it swilled over my tongue, down my throat and the spreading warmth as it settled in my stomach. Just one shot, just one, would solve all my problems.

I quashed the temptation by making a cup of instant coffee. As it went down I realised I had been sitting idle for far too long. I glanced at my watch. It was barely four o'clock. Would this day never end? Never have I known time to drag by so painfully before.

Suddenly I felt a change in the wind. It had swung round— at last, at long last—slightly and was now coming from the north-west. Still driving me mainly to the south, but at least I could pick up a fraction of that lost distance to the east. Like a fretting child I wondered now long ago it had changed. How much of it had I missed while so preoccupied with myself?

Feverishly I hauled in the sea anchor and found myself mar-
velling how the smallest slice of luck could change my whole
outlook. Only a minute before I had been feeling miserable,
angry, frustrated. Now I couldn't have felt better if the sun had
been shining and the temperature had been eighty degrees.
Even my feet began to feel better.

From then on I rowed solidly. Steady strokes and fairly long.
Silver skipped before the wind like a racing yacht. In, out, in,
out. On and on, hour after hour. My back bending forward and
backward with hardly a halt. I felt as if I could go on for ever.
And just as steadily the wind blew for me. It gradually increased
from about five miles an hour to ten, through fifteen until it
reached a constant 20 mph. It was like winning the top pools
prize, and I grimly determined to grab every possible advantage.

When I looked at my watch again it was dark. The luminous
dial was reading nearly one-thirty in the morning. Apart from
a pause for a hurried dinner, I had been rowing for about nine
hours. And I was sweating. In this deep freeze which had been
eating into my bones for so long I was sweating. I grinned with
joy to myself. As I shipped the oars I could feel it running down
my swollen face, rivulets of it sliding under my collar.

I wrapped a towel around my neck and with another dabbed
gently at my face and finally crawled into my sleeping bag. I
must have gone to sleep as soon as my eyes closed.

I don't know how long I slept, but when I woke it was still
dark. I lay there trying to drop off again and being prevented
from doing so by wondering what it was that roused me.
Through the fog of sleep that was still tugging at me I realised
it was the chugging of a ship's diesel engines. The steady throb
seemed to be coming from a long way off. But it was getting
louder. And still I did not move. I just lay there listening to that
sound moving towards me. I remember thinking: 'Oh Christ,
I'm whacked . . . I can't get up.' At the same time I delivered a
reprimand, lashing myself with a sneer: 'You're not tired.
You're just plain bloody lazy.'

Forcing myself out of the sleeping bag, I groped my way out
of the little shelter. I blinked out over the starboard gunwale . . .
nothing but darkness filled by that engine throb. Blearily I
switched my eyes to port and was instantly wide awake. Just

800 yards away was a ship. Her lights carved a hole in the darkness and she was heading towards me. I got a radar flare out of the watertight container and grabbed my flashlight. By the light of the torch I hurriedly made sure the flare was dry. When these flares explode they let off metal particles which in theory should be picked up on the approaching ship's radar . . . that is if a radar watch is being maintained. That depends on the size of the ship and if she has sufficient crew to set up a round-the-clock radar look-out.

The ship came on, filling the night with light and noise. *Silver* would be so much matchwood if we got a swipe from that monster. The ship was about 200 yards away when, as I was preparing to trigger off my flare, I suddenly realised I had misjudged her direction. She was going to pass me with plenty of room to spare. She swept by about 200 yards astern and *Silver* rocked in the wake. It was obvious that nobody on that ship was aware of my existence. It had been a scary moment and, now the danger had passed, it dawned on me that I could have flashed my torch on and off as a first line of defence. I could only suppose that I had been too intent on ensuring that my radar flare was dry, and picking the right moment to fire it.

It was apparent that there can be times when one can pay too much attention to detail, if that were indeed the case. On the other hand, it was equally, if not more so, apparent, that I had not been thinking quickly enough. It was plain that the question of whether or not the torch should have been used was now unimportant. What had infuriated me was that I had not even thought of using that torch so that I would then be able to make the decision of whether or not to use it. The decision should have been mine. It should not have been a matter of chance. For how many chances will the Atlantic allow one man?

While mentally kicking myself I watched the ship's lights fading away and it occurred to me, judging from the diesel note of the engine, that it could well be a fishing vessel. If it was, then it would be just possible that I was as far south as the Grand Banks. Here the depth of water varies between 80 and 100 fathoms and this shallowness allows the sunlight to penetrate the water and develop a vast crop of marine life. And it is here that great schools of herring and cod gather for feeding. It is easy to understand how this area became one of the world's greatest fishing grounds. That ship was the clue. But I wanted to be sure.

If I could pick up that ship on my two-way radio they would be able to give me my exact position . . . the first time I would have known it in eight days. Making a brief mental note of relief that my brain appeared to be ticking over properly once again, I unlashed the radio and tried to get it working. I tuned in and started rapping out the message which would have startled any ship's radio operator . . . if he had heard it.

'Row-boat *Super Silver* calling, row-boat *Super Silver* calling . . . come in, please; come in, please.'

But nobody heard me. I heard the Canadian coastguards receiving positions of ships at sea. Again I sent my message. Again no answer. Again those ships reporting to the coast-guards. All that activity somewhere out there in the darkness and nothing I could do.

But there was just one more shot in my locker. Perhaps the ship which had passed so close was also giving her position to the coastguards. Maybe, if I could pick her out because her call would be stronger than the rest, then I could gauge my own position from the information she sent to the coast.

Once again I tuned in. I picked up three more messages, but there was no distinctive difference in the strength of those messages. There was, however, one common denominator. The positions they gave were all roughly within fifty or so miles of each other. I must, I decided, be somewhere near the fishing grounds.

Making rough and ready calculations, I figured I had travelled some 200 miles and mainly on a southerly course. On that reckoning my drift to the east could not have been much more than a hundred miles. It was a depressing thought. I still had a hundred miles of this ice-box to cross before I came to its meeting point with the Gulf Stream, where usually the mixture of cool and warm waters produces a fog which is known as Arctic smoke. No matter how thick the fog, I knew I would not be really happy until I saw it.

By Tuesday morning, 27 May, I was still making crushingly

slow progress. I had awoken early. As I boiled the kettle an un-
real brightness gathered all around me. The greyness which
had dogged me for so many days was lifting. Up in the sky to
the east, a pale, watery sun was peeping at me, through a chink
in the usual spread of heavy cloud. The chink opened to a
crack and the sun seemed to hang there as if it had stopped.
Wispy clouds raced across it like the ends of a chiffon scarf
blowing over a pretty girl's face. Then it vanished for good, the
clouds once again taking over the entire world in their shroud
of lowering grey.

But it was a different day. A wonderful day. A look at the
thermometer showed me just how hard that sun was trying. The
temperature was 50°F the first time it had been so high since
the voyage began. From the north-west a 25-mph wind was
helping *Silver*, at least in part, towards the east. I hauled in
the sea anchor and let her have her head.

The time, the situation, the weather was right to deal at last
with the problem of my feet. I might not get another chance for
days. Tomorrow the Labrador could turn nasty again, plum-
meting the temperature to zero. Now that I had allowed myself to think of my feet again I realised they were so numb I
would not have felt a knife going into them. They were so
swollen it took about twenty minutes to ease my boots off. My
sainted aunt! They were in an unholy mess. The skin was
greyish white and wrinkled like pickled pork which had been
left far too long in the brine tub. And the skin had, in places,
peeled off my soles and heels. They were numb to the ankles
and so swollen that I thought they never would be the right
shape again. They looked useless and were useless. My great
consolation was that I was not on a march. What the hell was
I going to do?

I doubled over on the bottom of *Silver* and started trying to
squeeze some life back into them. I couldn't even feel the
touch of my own hands up to a point just below the ankles. As
I applied the pressure a little higher, coming into the area
where the blood was still trying to circulate, the pain was so
intense I snatched my hands away as if I had burned them.

Carefully I dried my feet thoroughly, put on a pair of dry
woollen socks and then wrapped them round with a thick

woollen sweater. One thing I knew for sure, I couldn't mess about with roughshod treatment this time. It would take a lot more than a few drops of oil from a sardine tin to get these ugly clumps of dead flesh into shape. I needed help. And there was only one place to which I could turn: the chapter headed 'Medical Problems in Cold Climates' in my medical bible.

I would advise that no prospective Atlantic rower should be without this book—*A Traveller's Guide to Health*. Written by Lieutenant-Colonel James M. Adam of the Royal Army Medical Corps, it is a compact directory to prevention, diagnosis and cure for travellers and explorers. I know it has helped many an adventurer through sticky patches and saved them from too much severe discomfort.

After reading the chapter I had to decide: 'Was I suffering from frostbite or the slightly minor form of exposure which is known as either 'immersion' or 'trench foot'? As I read the section devoted to frostbite, I had to chuckle. It said: 'The test of a true friend is to put feet in danger of frostbite on his abdomen to re-warm them.' I must confess I very much doubt if any chum of mine, had he been with me, would have allowed my feet within a mile of himself.

It was obvious that it didn't really matter whether I was suffering the first stages of frostbite or trench foot. Massage was out at all costs in both cases. If that pain had not shot through my ankles a few minutes before I would have been rubbing away like mad. I couldn't lie down in a warm place and couldn't go indoors as advised by Lieutenant-Colonel Adam, who, naturally, had not had lone Atlantic rowers in mind when he wrote this book. There was one conclusion applicable to either complaint. Keep the feet dry and keep them warm.

Uncovering them, I again dried them and then dug out three pairs of thick oiled wool seaman's stockings—I had brought about twenty pairs with me—and pulled them on one after the other. That, I thought, should handle the problem of keeping them warm. But how to keep them dry?

I couldn't get my boots on again. I was stumped for a while. It was while I was wondering how to keep my boots dry until I could use them again that I hit on the way to solve both problems. The heavy-duty plastic bags in which my rations were packed would be the perfect answer. They measured about one foot by two feet and I had a few spare ones on hand.

The boots were separately wrapped up, one to a bag, and then sealed down with masking tape. Now for my feet. I put the toes of my right foot into one corner of a bag and then meticulously wrapped the remainder of the bag around my leg up to the knee. This I held in place with strong elastic bands—I had seen these stout bands in a shop back in St Johns and bought a bundle, thinking vaguely that they were bound to be useful for something—which stopped above the ankle, giving the lower part of the bag a balloon effect around my foot. They looked as if they were floating in two huge air bubbles.

They looked utterly ridiculous. I held them up, examined them, waggled them and laughed my head off. Here I was wondering what I looked like and there was nobody to share the joke. I looked around. The wind was still from the northwest. It was still blowing for me. I felt great. Gulf Stream here I come.

4 | A pink elephant
28 May-2 June

I was rolled up into a tight ball like a cat trying to bury its paws and nose in its own coat. Sometime during the night I must have slid down inside my sleeping bag until my head was entirely covered. My knees were drawn up as high as I could get them, with my elbows tucked into my groin and my forearms pressed against my chest. My hands were cupped around my face with the little fingers meeting across my nose.

Each breath was a luxury. The warm air from my nostrils, trapped by my hands, momentarily rolled over my face before escaping. As I came to—that is the only way to describe it, for waking up had become more like breaking through a bout of unconsciousness—I kept my eyes shut and breathed harder and faster into my hands. The warmth was like a drug. For a few minutes I lay there without moving, thinking of nothing but the warm air on my face.

I slowly stretched until my head poked out of the top of the sleeping bag. Gingerly I opened my cupped hands without taking them from my face. The cold sliced across my raw flesh like a knife. I discovered later that my guess that the temperature was at about freezing point was only four degrees out. Hurriedly I recupped my hands back into position and lay there opening and shutting them to acclimatise myself to the chill dawn.

Even through the thickness of my Portuguese mittens I could feel the bristles of my beard rustling with each movement. I had not shaved, or washed, since leaving St Johns. I was still wearing the same shirt, the same underclothing. All I had managed to do in the pursuit of cleanliness was to clean my teeth.

Salt crystals had begun to gather in every corner of flesh. They rubbed against my neck, rustled under my armpits and merrily crackled away in far more uncomfortable spots. I promised myself a thorough bath and change of clothing at the very first alteration in the weather.

Finally I reached forward to pull aside a corner of the canvas hanging in front of my shelter to look at the new day. A new day? Once again there was no change. Overhanging cloud, slate-coloured seas, the horizon hidden in mist and only the seagulls for company. How maddening those birds are! They sit in the icy water bobbing about like corks and looking as if they are revelling in a warm bath.

It was full daylight, if this eternal greyness could be described as such. But there was something different about this morning, after all. The tangy smell of the sea was not nearly so strong. In fact there was a completely different fragrance in the air. It was the smell of curry. Strong, spicy and, even at 7 am, mouth-watering. I sniffed at it like a hungry tramp. At first I thought my imagination must be playing tricks. It was, I figured, a sort of mental mirage. Yet it did not fade. The more I sniffed, the stronger became the smell of curry. I knew I wouldn't rest until I had tracked it down.

Down on my knees in the shelter, I rummaged around. Out went my sleeping bag. Out went the air mattress—which I no longer bothered to blow up—and out went practically everything. Then I found it . . . a broken jar of curry paste. When it was broken, how it was broken, there was no way of knowing. To me it was a sort of minor tragedy. My near-obsessive liking for curry was born when I was serving in Malaya. I eat it in one form or another nearly every day when I'm ashore. I had chosen it as my staple diet for my Atlantic trip.

I was carrying a hundred days of SAS field rations. Each day's pack has been scientifically selected by Army diet specialists and contains enough calories to keep a hard-working man going for a whole day. One pack contains three brews of tea, complete with sugar and powdered milk. There is a porridge block which can be eaten as a biscuit or boiled up to normal breakfast consistency by adding boiling water. There are plain biscuits and a tube of margarine, a tin of cheese, a tin of sardines, two Mars bars and a slab of chocolate. There are matches and salt, toilet paper, vitamin tablets and a can-opener.

And, of course, the most important item of all . . . the main course. This is a large block of dehydrated curry plus a little rice and a few raisins. Each pack weighs about one and a half pounds. With so much curry on board little *Silver*, most people would probably wonder why I should worry about one broken jar of curry paste. After all, there were three more jars amongst my supplies.

The curry paste was a luxury, an added goodie, but, even more vital, an emergency food supply. It had already come in useful when the weather had been too bad for me to cook. Eaten by the spoonful straight from the jar, I had reckoned it would give me warmth and stamina in tight spots.

To say I was dismayed would perhaps be overestimating this ridiculous little drama. But I was upset. I cleaned up the mess and dumped the broken jar overboard. Then I set about re-packing the remaining three jars as if they were thin-shelled eggs. Each one was wrapped in about two or three inches of clothing and then wedged tightly into a plastic box which I then lashed against the boat's side in a far corner of my shelter. I shook it, tugged at it and was not satisfied until there was absolutely no sign of movement either inside or outside the box.

As time passed I was beginning to realise that no matter what happened there was usually some compensatory factor. Even the episode of the lost curry paste had its good point. The mental concentration used in tracing the smell; the first moments of slight panic; the feeling of frustration and finally the steps taken to ensure there were no repeats . . . all this had completely driven from my mind thoughts of the weather, my feet or my position. If only one can keep busy enough—difficult enough in such a small space—there is no time left for self-pity.

I followed up my home-spun philosophy with immediate action. A cup of tea and cheese and biscuits for breakfast and by 7.45 am I had the oars out and started rowing. At least the wind was with me. I was heading south-east with a following wind of about 15 mph. I rowed for three or four hours. Perhaps more, perhaps less. I have no idea exactly how long I rowed that day. It did not seem to matter how long I rowed just so long as I did row.

There was a tremendous satisfaction in getting the oars into the water again. In, out; body forward, then back; stretching, pulling, bending like a man possessed. It was almost as if I was driven by the wild thought that I could reach a British shore that very day. *Silver* behaved like a dream, sliding through the water, calm and steady. She seemed to be urging me on, telling me, 'If only you will row I'll get you out of this Labrador icebox'.

I was only too anxious to comply. The sound of the water rippling along *Silver*'s sides was like music. The sense of movement was exciting. The feel of the wind blowing into my face stimulated and refreshed me. As I bent and pulled, I was filled with a new determination. It could be done and I would do it. Frozen feet, blistered hands, aching bones, soaked to the skin and without the slightest clue to my position—none of those hampering circumstances was going to hold me up any longer.

When competing in a running race while in the Army I had made up my mind to win or literally drop in the attempt. That had been during my early days of service. I won the race and dropped after passing the tape. From then on my personal philosophy was simple but effective: 'Win or bust.' As I heaved at the oars, I ran that race again and vividly saw every step like a cine film in my brain. The effect was almost hypnotic. Like a slave master standing in the stern of a galley, I began pacing my rowing time. With each stroke of the oars I breathed: 'Win ... or bust. ... Win ... or bust. ... Win ... or bust.'

Painted on the bows of *Silver* was the SAS badge and motto: 'Who dares wins.' I could see the blue outline sometimes as *Silver*'s nose rose to the swell. 'Well,' I told myself, 'you've dared, now start winning.' I mentally thrashed myself along for hours. I don't know how long I rowed that day. Time held no meaning at all. Only distance, and plenty of it, counted.

Not until the late afternoon did I notice that *Silver* was beginning to toss and turn again. The wind had built up and was slapping her at about 40 mph and growing stronger all the time. But it did not matter too much. For it was holding steady from the north-west and kept *Silver* moving in roughly the right direction.

Not until I had lashed the oars inboard and set about making a meal did I remember that after sorting out the broken curry jar in the morning I had slipped and fallen against the cooker.

In my fall I broke off the door of the cylindrical windshield. I figured I would be able to mend it all right, but not right then. Crouching in front of the opening left by the broken door, I shielded the gas jets with my body. It did the trick, but I knew that I could not continue in that way every day. The door would have to be repaired as soon as possible.

There was one last decision to make before bedding down. Should the sea anchor go out or not? The wind had shown signs of swinging round and there was a chance that during the night it would come right round until it was blowing me back over the precious distance I had covered. Yet if it did not change, the sea anchor would slow down whatever advantage the wind provided. It was time for a gamble and I decided to take a chance. I kept the sea anchor inboard.

After a rather uncomfortable night I woke on 29 May to find the wind had made a fool of me. It was blowing strongly from completely the other, the wrong, direction. Luckily for my peace of mind, I would never know whether or not I had lost my gamble. I would never know whether the change had been so recent that it had made virtually no difference to my progress. Mooning over a question to which I would never find an answer was a complete waste of time. I cut it out of my mind and did the only thing possible—put out the sea anchor.

Checking the temperature later, I found it had risen to 38°F. Maybe I was fooling myself, I don't know, but I drew great consolation from that reading. I reckoned it was evidence that my gamble had paid off, after all; that I had made good distance and was actually edging into a warmer area.

Patting *Silver*'s gunwale as if it were a pet dog, I grinned with delight and said: 'Good girl, you're a good girl.' Maybe *Silver* felt I was becoming a little too cocksure and decided to give me a sharp lesson. I stepped over the seat to reach for a fresh pack of rations but I did not step far enough. I committed what I consider to be the cardinal sin of a lone sailor when moving about his small craft: to be caught without both feet firmly planted on the deck.

Stretching towards the ration pack, I judged I could reach it by leaning forward just another six inches. To manage this I should have put both feet over the seat. Instead, I allowed the back foot to rise above the deck as I bent outward and downward. As my hand grasped the top of the pack, *Silver*, caught by an awkward wave, heeled over. I fought for my balance. My raised foot instinctively stabbed down towards the deck as I tried to straighten up. Idiotically I still retained my grip on the ration pack. But as my foot went down, the force of it meeting the deck jarred my ultra-sensitive ankle. There was no sense of feeling in the foot itself, but the pain just above the ankle was murderous. It felt as if I had snapped my foot off right at that point.

Straddled across the seat as I was, there was nothing I could do. I knew my eyes were watering with the pain and I was cursing at the top of my voice. But *Silver* was still heeling over; still moving in one direction; tipping the deck until it was angled at about forty-five degrees.

One again my back foot jabbed down towards the deck and this time I forced myself to keep it there as I struggled to lean in the opposite direction to *Silver*. And still she went over. With a sudden rush I felt myself falling towards the water, helpless and utterly out of control.

Although the whole episode could not have taken more than a few seconds, everything was as clear as a sharp photograph. As the water seemed to rise to meet me, I let go of the ration pack and watched it splash into the sea. *Silver* was still moving over and just one more inch would have had my feet completely off the deck. But I couldn't know for sure, for my feet were still numb. My position had to be judged solely by the angle and the feeling of tension in my calves, thighs and hips.

As I fell I grabbed madly for the gunwale. In that split second I knew I had misjudged my timing. The right hand slid right over the gunwale, missing it by a hair. I felt the palm of my left hand slap hard against a firm object. It was the handle of the water pump. What incredible luck! But for that I would have been straight over the side. My reflexes, thank goodness, were working overtime. At the moment of touch, my fingers locked around that handle, so tightly that nothing but a knife would have loosened them, and my arm stiffened into a desperate bar of straining muscle.

At the same moment my right hand had scrabbled back in-

E

board and clamped itself over the edge of the gunwale. The jerk as I checked my headlong rush, half-slung me over the side, leaving me hanging out, as far as my waistline, over the water. My face was just a couple of inches above the water and *Silver*'s gunwale had heeled over so far that I could feel the water splashing over my right hand. As I hung there my head was dunked by a passing wave, leaving me spluttering and dripping. Then, with maddening slowness, *Silver* gradually righted herself. Panic over.

Sitting on the floorboards to regain my breath, I found myself quivering from head to toe. I thanked my lucky stars I had only my head to dry. Admittedly I was wearing my safety harness and if I had gone over I should have been able to pull myself back aboard. But a full bodily soaking in that icy Labrador Current was the last thing I needed. The thought of having to strip down to the buff in a temperature only six degrees above freezing did not strike me as very funny at all. I tested the water temperature. It was 32°F—freezing point. How long could I last in that?

Yet I was fated that day—destined to get a soaking and nothing was going to stop me getting it. And this time it was funny. For the Atlantic, so to speak, caught me bending. Performing one's natural functions was a tricky affair at the best of times. A plastic bucket and a peaceful moment was the most one could hope for. This time I had only the plastic bucket. There I was with my pants down and along came another freak wave. I had my back to it and therefore had no warning as it curled up and rose to splash down right over me. It is difficult to say which is the greater shock, the sudden wave of cold that swept over my entire body or the unexpected impact of several gallons of water hitting me in the backside so hard it knocked me off my feet. Believe me, that water was brass-monkey cold and gave me instant teeth-chatter.

I could afford to laugh this time. At least I was *inside Silver*. I had not been in such an incongruous situation since accidentally being shot in the groin when serving in the Middle East. The bullet emerged through my left buttock and, apart from thinking I had been ruined for life, it was weeks before I could sit down properly. It is moments like these when one can truly appreciate some of the simpler comforts of life.

So it was a strip to the buff, after all. If a ship had come along then, I wonder what the crew would have made of the sight of a naked, unshaven and apparently wild man asking if they would be kind enough to direct him to the nearest British beach. I must have looked like a refugee from the cast of *Hair*.

I dried and changed in record time. Nevertheless, my body was a mass of goose pimples long before I had finished dressing. By then I was trembling as violently as a leaf being battered by a rainstorm. Racing through an exercise session, I then un-lashed the oars and got stuck into a couple of hours' rowing.

Another bitterly cold night had to be faced—and an uncom-fortable one. Winds, swinging steadily round to the east, built up throughout the night to more than 50 mph. *Silver* bounced and quivered and shipped water by the hundredweight. Stand-ing by the pumps all night caused a great loss of sleep, but at least it kept me warm. By the morning the wind had shifted completely and was blowing directly from the east at about 60 mph.

Yet again I was being blown back on my course. Yet again I was losing precious distance yard by hard-won yard. I groaned with angry frustration. 'Will this bloody shuttlecock existence never finish?' I felt as if I had been chasing up and down the same stretch of ocean for days. And each grey day had been frustratingly so much like the other. The only change had been the size of the waves and the ever-changing wind.

Once again I was lying down in the bottom of *Silver* with my back jammed against one side but within reaching distance of the pumps. St Johns radio station could still be heard loud and clear and that added to the depressing impression that I was making little headway. Listening to the newscast it seemed to me that they thought I was a goner.

The report was short. 'Lone Atlantic rower Tom McClean has not been sighted since setting out from St Johns two weeks ago. It is most likely that he has met some severe weather con-ditions, but so far he has apparently not used his radio. Neither the coastguards nor ships in the general area have reported hearing from him. Shipping experts believe it likely that he is in between the normal shipping lanes and this would explain why he has not been seen.'

Maybe I was a little oversensitive, but I couldn't help feeling that what those shipping experts were really saying was: 'McClean is a bloody nuisance as well as a bloody fool.' To worry about what other people thought of me right then wasn't going to help my morale. I shrugged my shoulders. 'Not to worry,' I told myself, 'just keep going.'

The last thing in the world I wanted was for anybody to get concerned about me, but I must confess I yearned to see a ship just to find out what progress I had made. Having been without sun I had been unable to take a sight and during the rough weather it had been impossible to use my plotting board, firstly because I couldn't keep it steady enough and secondly because I did not want it to get soaked.

Navigation had really become quite a problem. My rough calculations were unsatisfactory but were the best I could do. I reckon I must have made between fifty and a hundred miles in a more or less due easterly direction before those maddening winds turned me on to what I was sure was a due south course. Deciding how far I had travelled south was pure guesswork. It could have been anything between 100 and 200 miles—but no good to me.

Although I didn't like to be too sure in case of later bitter disappointment, I felt that at some point in the last couple of days or so I had been heading in an easterly direction, thus completing the last leg of a huge zig-zag pattern.

The break I had been needing came the next morning. I woke at 4.30 am to find a steady 10 mph wind breezing along from the north-west. Beautiful. In fact, almost perfect. I celebrated with a breakfast of biscuits and Marmite, followed by biscuits and strawberry jam and tea. Then I placed a bar of chocolate within easy reach and got cracking with the rowing.

What a day! What an absolutely marvellous day! I started rowing just before 5 am and went right through until 9 pm. Sixteen beautiful hours of heading east with that wonderful north-west wind never rising above 15 mph. I stopped only for lunch and several cups of coffee. So important was it to take every possible advantage of the best conditions I had so far encountered that I decided I couldn't waste such vital minutes, even for coffee. I worked out a scheme whereby I did not need to stop rowing completely while I drank.

Shipping the oars inboard, I left them in the rowlocks and then leaned forward to put the kettle on. Then I grabbed the oars and got in a few more strokes while waiting for the kettle to boil. Inboard with the oars again, make the coffee, take a few sips and jam the cup in a tight corner while continuing to row. Then I repeated the process until the cup was empty.

Maybe the coffee got cold, but that didn't matter. Maybe the plan sounded cock-eyed but that didn't matter either. What did matter was that, true or false, it gave me the great feeling that not a single moment was being thrown away. I felt happier than at any time since the trip began. The Army has a phrase which describes perfectly how I felt: 'I was chuffed, oh boy, was I chuffed!' Just a few more days like this would make all the difference.

My wishes came true the next morning, Sunday, 1 June. It was almost too good to believe. That 10 to 15 mph wind from the north-west was still behind me. I woke at about six-thirty. That surprised me a little, as I had planned on making another start before daylight. But I suppose yesterday's effort must have taken more out of me than I realised. My hands were certainly feeling the effect. They ached from wrist to finger-tips and were almost too stiff to bend. I could hear them crack as I massaged them, trying to restore them to some state of suppleness. It was vital that my hands did not pack in now, so I decided to start rowing a little later to give them a chance to regain some strength.

In the meantime I pulled out one of my Sunday letters. It was from Val and June, the girls on the switchboard at the SAS base in Hereford. I could picture them clearly in my mind's eye. Both pretty, both with gorgeous smiles and both kind and considerate. Pretty girls have always been quite a weakness of mine and it struck me that this was the first time I had thought of a girl since setting out. Frankly I was astonished. I hadn't even glanced at the girlie magazine somebody had thrown into the boat at St Johns. Lone rowing can certainly keep a man's mind well occupied. It was just as well, for it would be a long time before I would be dating anybody again.

My thoughts reminded me of a small mystery which I had forgotten in the rush of getting ready for the row. Just before leaving England I had received a postcard picturing a lucky black cat and bearing the message: 'You won't remember me, but I met you on a train travelling from London to Hereford and you told me all about your boat. Good luck, Paula.' There was no address.

Who was Paula? What did she look like? What drivel had I been spouting? I tried going back over every train journey I had made in the past few months. But I could not remember Paula. I felt a little sad and a little guilty, for one should be able to remember someone kind enough to think of you. But it seemed there were quite a lot of people thinking of me. Suddenly I felt quite lonely under the grey clouds and surrounded by that slate-coloured sea. I grinned sheepishly at my reflections on my determination never to be tangled up by being involved emotionally with anybody; my dedication to being a loner. The words of the song ran through my mind: 'People who need people . . . are the luckiest people in the world.' Maybe that is right. Maybe one cannot be a loner all through life.

Right then that letter from Val and June was the best company in the world. It began with a little prayer: 'May the Good Lord keep you safe.' He had certainly been doing a fine job of that so far. I had come through some pretty bad patches and was still all in one piece.

Val and June reminded me that an old pal had given me a small plastic pink elephant for luck. I had forgotten about that too. It was packed away somewhere aboard *Silver*. I had a quick search but without luck. Pinky the elephant became quite important. I wanted to find it. Torn between superstition—for I really thought of it as a lucky mascot—and the need to start rowing, I plumped for the rowing. That wind was too good to waste any longer.

To be perfectly honest, I was also a trifle apprehensive of allowing myself to get maudlin. Deliberately sarcastic, I told myself: 'Hell, you'll be crying in your beer before you know where you are!'

The pain of rowing was a perfect antidote. Yesterday's burst of action had eaten deep into my hands. Each pull on the oars stretched my fingers until the very joints seemed to be coming apart. Giving in would have been so easy. The temptation to kid myself that I needed a rest was hard to resist. But I couldn't, I wouldn't, allow myself to just sit through such perfect conditions. For nearly half an hour I rowed with my eyes screwed up with the effort and my teeth gritting into each other. It took about that long for the pain to wear away . . . or was it just a case of getting used to it?

At times I would swear that I was only partly conscious. But at last the pain began to fade. Sweat was pouring down my face and swimming into my now open eyes. Stopping to wipe it away would be fatal. I was sure I would never have the guts to start again. 'Row, you stupid bastard, row,' I snarled. I blinked and shook my head to get rid of the surplus perspiration and by the end of another half-hour felt somewhere near normal once again. I chanced a short pause to wipe my face and wrap a towel round my neck and started again.

That hour of near agony was well worth while. Once I could take things in it was a delight to see how *Silver* was fairly zipping along. Just like the day before, I kept her stern directly in line with the wind, and that, with the waves, gave her a surfing movement.

Monday, 2 June, began as another perfect day. A concerted search for Pinky located him tucked away in a plastic container together with my fishing gear. Would there ever be a day when I would be able to use that gear? The idea had been to provide myself with a little fresh food now and again. I tied Pinky firmly to the side of the compass with nylon parachute cord. It was quite extraordinary how much better I felt for that simple little exercise. Luck, I felt, was with me now, but I couldn't leave it as a sole responsibility for Pinky.

I nailed a St Christopher medal to the roof of my shelter and alongside it went a Canadian one-cent piece given me by a well-wishing Newfoundlander. I could see that array of lucky charms from my rowing position. I chuckled to myself: 'What a superstitious idiot you've turned out to be.' But, after all, it is legendary that most sailors are inclined to be superstitious, so I felt I was in good company.

Perhaps lucky charms take some time to become effective,

for no sooner were they all in position than the winds began building up again. I managed to keep rowing for a bit, but eventually it proved too dangerous to remain sitting up. My comfortable days were over for the time being. That was obvious.

By midday a savage north-wester was lashing the seas into mountainous waves. Before packing in the day's rowing stint I had just sat there, watching the beginnings of the storm racing towards *Silver*'s stern like white-topped walls of grey slate. Each wall grew larger, higher and faster as I watched. From my 'safety' position on the floorboards I hurriedly boiled up a curry lunch and a mug of tea. 'This blow,' I told myself, 'is no short-term job.' I reckoned I could be stuck on the floorboards of *Silver* for three or four days. It seemed to be set for a hurricane.

The wind came howling over the side of *Silver*, tearing at anything that was loose, rattling my cooking pans like a BBC sound-effects studio man trying to simulate the sound of a huge kitchen. The canvas draped over the front of my shelter was snatched into the air and cracked like an angry stock-whip. Crawling around on my hands and knees, I checked all lashings and tied down everything that showed the least sign of movement. There was nothing to do after that except crawl back to my position by the pumps, wedge myself in and stand by to pump when needed.

My God! It was a nightmare of a night. *Silver* pitched and rolled as if deliberately trying to throw me overboard. She seemed to have developed a sudden frenzied hate for me personally. There was no sleep at all. *Silver* shipped water all through the night. I pumped, I bailed and I clung to her like a limpet. There were moments, I am sure, when she was completely out of the water. I could feel those waves carry her high into the air as if trying to throw us up into the black void overhead.

Then suddenly the wave would chop itself away from under *Silver*, leaving her hanging in mid-air. Then she would drop. The sense of falling was terrific. It was probably no more than a few inches. It seemed like yards. When *Silver* hit the water again I literally bounced on the floorboards. These sickening thuds seemed to be threatening to split *Silver* apart at every seam. Every time I clung to whatever I could get hold of, and every time it seemed that I would be torn loose and thrown into the teeth of that screeching wind and swirled away into the darkness like a helpless leaf.

Within the first five minutes of that storm I must have been soaked through to the skin. And throughout the night there was a constant level of water in *Silver* which, I am sure, I never managed to get below a foot deep. I just had to lie in it and fight for survival in a world that had gone stark, staring crazy.

My arms ached, my body was bruised and aching and my head rang with the din of the storm. Experts who had experienced the Atlantic in all her moods had warned me it would be rough at times. I had known it would be rough. I had already experienced an angry Atlantic. But neither my experience nor my imagination had ever stretched to the vicious savagery of this punishing night.

Looking back now, I try to tell myself I was not afraid. I wonder. I certainly do not recall being afraid at the time. Scared, yes. But fear which hits you in the pit of your stomach; fear of dying; fear which paralyses the brain and the muscles? No, I don't think so. On the other hand, a man can be afraid of being afraid.

I do know that I started talking, or rather yelling, to myself during those murderously tormenting hours. I screamed it out against the fury of the storm: 'You'll be all right. You'll get there. Stick it out . . . for Christ's sake just stick it out.'

Stick it out I did. But not entirely by myself. I have never been a great churchgoer, but that night I prayed. It was simple and straightforward: 'Help me see this through, please help me fight.' That's all. A few words which I addressed in the general direction of the sky. When you are alone under these conditions it gives strength to think there is someone greater watching over you.

5 | Into the Gulf
3-8 June

I had been wrong. The storm did not last three or four days. By Tuesday morning, 3 June, it had begun to blow itself out. I had never before been so thankful to be so utterly wrong. I was still sitting my the pumps as dawn rose. I had not shut my eyes all night. Exhaustion, sheer complete exhaustion, seemed only a breath away. The mere thought of moving was a monumental effort in itself. But move I had to.

I forced myself on to my knees to light the cooker and brew some tea. The hot tea almost scalded my throat as I swallowed. I started as my throat burned. It was the first quick movement I'd made in the last ten minutes. I drank deeply again, stinging myself into action with the smarting pain of the hot liquid. Slowly I felt myself coming back to life.

Miserable I might be. Cold, wet and battered I might be. But I was a long way from finished. I started singing, it was more of a croak actually, *Scottish Soldier*. After the first two lines the words dried up. I had forgotten the words of one of my favourite songs. Not that words mattered right then. I hummed my way through the rest of the song in a tuneless, rasping mumble. Once I had finished I started again. Four times I hummed my way through that song.

With my hands clasped round a second mug of tea, I sat on the seat waiting for my breakfast to cook. Until this morning, no matter what happened, the all-important thing to me had been to row for as long as I could at every opportunity, even if it meant going without proper food. But last night's storm had changed all that. Food had become absolutely vital. I boiled up two of my dried porridge cakes and added a liberal helping of condensed milk. This was followed by a half-pound of dry biscuits heavily smeared with strawberry jam. It was the first time during the trip that I had eaten until I felt utterly full.

As I ate I contemplated the eternal greyness of sea and sky

which had dogged me practically every yard of the way. Even the wildlife seemed to be giving this depressing Atlantic the cold shoulder. I had seen very few birds during the past seventeen days.

I had not seen a fish, a shark or a porpoise. Nor had I seen a ship. At the thought of a ship I peered long and carefully around the horizon, going through every point of the compass until my eyes were back where they had started, staring over *Silver*'s bow. Nothing. I knew there would be nothing. I knew there would be nothing when I looked again. But it did not stop me. My eyes scraped every yard of the sea between *Silver* and the horizon once more. Far to the east and high in the sky I spotted four birds. They were heading east. I wondered if they were heading for Britain and how long the journey would take. All I could think of was that if they were heading for Britain they would be there a long, long time ahead of me. For the first time the loneliness began to hit me.

Should I have made this a double-handed trip? I wondered. Would a companion have eased the situation? Would somebody to talk to, to joke with, have made my troubles seem any the less? If I had been able to talk over the problems of the Atlantic would it have helped to solve them?

Fleetingly it seemed that a chum in *Silver* would have made all the difference in the world. But this wishful thinking was a purely academic exercise. The whole purpose of my adventure was to do it alone. To do it any other way would have no purpose at all. Chay and Ridge had already pulled off the double in great style. My job was the single-handed voyage and I had to get on with it. At least I had only myself to worry about.

Not quite only myself! There was *Silver*. Perhaps she couldn't get concerned about my welfare, but I could worry about her, and right then she looked a mess. After the hell of the night's storm all I had done was to indulge myself in a sort of self-pity. I had not given a thought to the tough little dory which had so gallantly carried me through hours of ocean fury.

There was about six inches of water swilling around on her floorboards. Dirty water which had developed a sort of frothy scum as the force of the storm had sloshed it around in the bottom of *Silver*. There were strands of seaweed scattered about.

Everything that would absorb moisture was dripping wet. Items of my supplies which were covered with heavy-duty plastic seemed to be okay. Drops of water covered every plastic package, but, when I opened two or three to check, everything inside was still perfectly dry.

My sleeping bag, my air bed and a sweater I had thoughtlessly left lying in my shelter were sopping. I lashed all three across the roof of the shelter, leaving just enough looseness for the wind to get underneath them, in an effort to dry them out. I pumped out the last six inches of water and threw the bits of seaweed overboard. That was about all I could do for *Silver* right then, but she looked a lot better.

The wind had dropped to a steady 15 mph and I started rowing to the south-east. But not for long. By the early afternoon the wind and sea started building up again. I shipped the oars, lashed them down and sat there looking at that empty scene once again.

All at once it wasn't empty any more. In the distance to the north-east I spotted the outline of a ship. It was miles away and looked no larger than a toy, but to me it was like a block of flats filling that wide open space. After days of absolutely nothing it was a strange feeling to think that there were actually people over there. Talking, laughing, singing people. No doubt people who would be only too willing to take me aboard and give me the run of all the comforts that were on board. A bath with piping hot water. What a luxury, a superb, blissful luxury to wallow and soak in that bath and let all my aches and pains ooze away.

They would offer me hot food, perhaps with fresh vegetables. They might even have fresh fruit and cream. Tinned cream, no doubt, but still cream. Then to a bed with a mattress, to lie between clean white sheets in a warm cabin protected on all four sides from the piercing fingers of the Atlantic winds.

They might have a doctor with pills, lotions and unctions to treat my feet, my blisters, my salt sores . . . such a dream. The ship was not heading anywhere near me and there was obviously no chance at all of them spotting me from that distance. And just as well. I wondered if I could have withstood the temptation of such an invitation. Could I? There was no telling. I told myself that I would be able to do so; that I would decline all offers with thanks and simply ask for a check on my position. To be perfectly honest, I had my doubts. The real test was just three or four hours away.

The afternoon started as a complete waste of time. The wind was too strong for me to think of rowing, yet not strong enough for *Silver* to ship water in dangerous quantities. I suppose if I had really wanted to do anything I could have found a dozen small chores to tackle. Most important, I should have looked at my feet. But I was tired—and probably a little idle also—and I told myself it would do me good to rest maybe even to snatch a doze.

Certainly, once that ship had passed out of sight, I became weary of looking at nothing but the empty sea. Propped up against my folded inflatable dinghy, I watched the thin steel rod of *Silver*'s radio mast tracing a constant rolling pattern against the grey clouds as we rolled and pitched.

I watched the tip of that mast for ages, trying to judge how many inches each pattern would be out of line with the next. For a while I was far away from the Atlantic; far away from this ever-moving water; far, far away amongst green fields listening to the soothing sounds of the English countryside in the summertime. Every yard of the Venns' farm near Aylesbury came to me as clearly as if I were there. I walked over those fields taking in the growing crops, patted cattle and even chased a broody group of hens as I had done when I was a youngster there.

It was the time of the year for mowing and the sweet smell of newly cut hay lingered in the Atlantic as precious as any exclusive Paris perfume. I walked miles. Across fields, over hills, through woods, into the surrounding villages and back again to the Venns' farmhouse for the sort of tea which only Mrs Venn knew how to set before a hungry man.

The thought of tea cut my dream. I switched on the radio, tuned into St Johns and lit the cooker. This time there was no mention of myself on the news broadcast. Well, I figured, that is better than hearing them say that they were losing hope of seeing me again.

I was hunched up in front of the cooker, squatting on my haunches listening to the music, when it happened. It was the sound of a bell, loud and distinct, right behind me. For a few seconds I didn't move a muscle. I just perched there, frozen into that one position, absolutely unable to believe the message my ears were pounding through to my brain.

I turned round and there was a fishing vessel almost on top of me. She was about twenty-five yards off my port side, so close I could read her name painted on the bow, *Rio Alfusqueiro*. I just stood and stared, hypnotised by my first sight of moving, waving human beings since—how long was it? A hundred years? Not quite three weeks and yet it was as if I had stepped into another world. For the first time in my life I got some idea of how Alice must have felt as she walked through that crazy looking glass.

They were lined along the rails, shouting and waving. They too must have been away from home for some time. They were unshaven and salt-crusted. Tough, sturdy, swarthy Portuguese fishermen looking like a bunch of villainous but jolly pirates. Some wore the traditional Portuguese stocking caps of wool, the tassel dangling rakishly down the right-hand side of the face. I almost glanced at their masthead to see if the Skull and Crossbones was flying there.

They were a wonderful, wonderful sight. As the *Rio*'s bridge drew level with me, I heard the skipper yelling at me in broken English: 'Hey! you all right, eh? You want anytink, eh? Help maybe? You in trouble, eh?'

By this time I had grabbed my chart and, waving it at him with one hand, I drew a cross in the air with the other hand in an effort to indicate to him that I wanted my position. And at the same time I was yelling: 'My position, Captain? Can you give me my position? Where . . . are . . . we?'

He waved as if he understood, but the *Rio* just steamed slowly past me. At first I thought he was ignoring me, that they had called out to me just for a spot of fun. 'Blimey,' I spluttered aloud, 'the bastard doesn't care. The lousy, rotten stinking pig!'

Almost at the same moment I spotted that his trawl was still out. He had steamed off to pull it inboard. Once that was done, he turned and steamed back on my port side, once again protecting me from the swell. We rolled there together no more than twenty yards apart, me with a hand cupped round my ear trying to catch what the *Rio*'s skipper was bawling through his cupped hands.

Then I got it. 'Poseeshun is 46°54′N, 47°24′W,' yelled the *Rio*'s captain. Then he asked again: 'Maybe you want food or water, eh?'

I bawled back: 'No thanks.'

'Then you want sometink else, maybe?' he bellowed.

'No thanks,' I replied, 'nothing but my poseeshun. And thanks a lot, Captain.'

We parted with the gap between us slowly widening. The crew still lined the rails. They had been grinning spectators of that little interchange between me and their skipper. Many of them were giving me the Churchill salute and, I hasten to add, it was the right way round.

I waved back with both arms way above my head. But it didn't seem enough to express the tremendous elation I was feeling. Suddenly I had an inspiration. I dived into my shelter, dug out a bottle of rum and then, gesturing towards them to wish them good luck, I took a great swig from the neck of the bottle. The roar of approval from the Portuguese came rolling across the water.

It was a strange little ceremony, but what a difference it made to me. My weariness had vanished. I was once again as full of battle as a fighting cock. And now it was over I realised I had passed the test without even thinking about it. I had refused all help and I had not had to force myself to do it. In fact the refusal had come as naturally as asking a chum to have a drink. I had done it without a single shaky doubt rearing its ugly head.

Just to cap it off, I at last knew exactly where I was: 46°54′N, 47°24′W. Just about 350 miles south-east of St Johns. Oh brother! I was really chuffed. I had beaten what I thought to be the worst part of the trip and must be, had to be, impossible not to be, on the edge of that Holy Grail of a Gulf Stream.

My luck had changed, I was sure of it. Now all I asked was two or three easy-going days with friendly breezes to give me a chance to sort myself out. And I got it. Was anybody, any-where, ever quite so lucky? Those days, long, long days when the air temperature never rose above 40°F and the water never above 35°F, were over. I had won the first round.

For four solid days and nights the wind became my ally. From the west it came with hardly a change of course. Nursing me, coaxing me, coddling me in one great swooping surge to the east and never rising much above 25 mph or falling below 10 mph. In the air there was warmth so distinct that my ice-capped brain actually imagined it could be touched. But there was no doubt about it—it could be felt. I was escaping from the freezing embrace of the Labrador Current and I swore I would never set eyes on that area of natural savagery ever again.

The yards, the miles, were spinning away with the water rippling and creaming away from *Silver*'s bows in the shape of a huge arrow-head. As *Silver* ate up the distance, so the temperature rose degree by degree, climbing gradually all the time, day by day, until it hit the all-time high so far: 48°F.

Everything was so perfect, so intoxicating; it had an almost sexy quality, like a capricious girl apologising for hitting you in the face with a flat iron and now suggesting that all should be forgiven and forgotten. And like any sucker for a pretty face I was only too ready to forgive, but I could never forget. I was alert, wary, suspicious and ready for the next blow. My guard would never drop.

By comparison with what I had experienced, these four days were like booking into a five-star hotel on the Côte d'Azur. But I had learned something during the past three weeks. It was a vital lesson, and hardship and danger had been my tutors. No matter how perfect the conditions and weather, no matter how calm the sea, I must never relax completely. I had said I would learn the hard way. I had.

Despite the discomfort that I had endured, I was truly glad that the opening stage of the journey had not been easy enough to tempt me into thinking the whole thing was going to be a cakewalk. Neither was I now going to be tempted into kidding myself that I had taken everything the Atlantic could throw at me. I deeply suspected that it had an abundant supply of dirty tricks still to play.

Chay Blyth and John Ridgway had spoken at great length

Teamwork

Super Silver's covered stern area and canvas awning gave scanty but vital protection from the weather

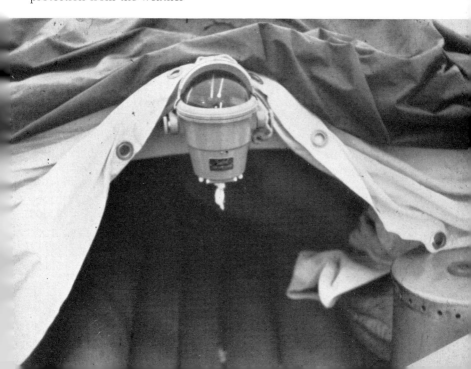

The hose from the all-important bilge pump was lashed over the spare oars to facilitate rapid repairs

Though feather-light, a space blanket retains 80 per cent of the body heat—and I needed all the warmth I could get

Sometimes the sea could be beautiful—*Silver* really did leave a silver wake

Waterproofing for my frost-bitten feet—those polythene bags were invaluable

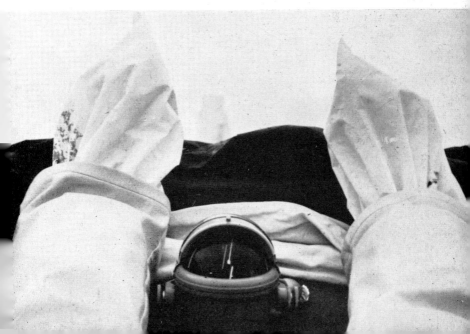

Keeping the log

Even in mid-Atlantic, a
good shave can be a
morale-booster

Inspecting my emergency fishing tackle

Silver looking very lived-in

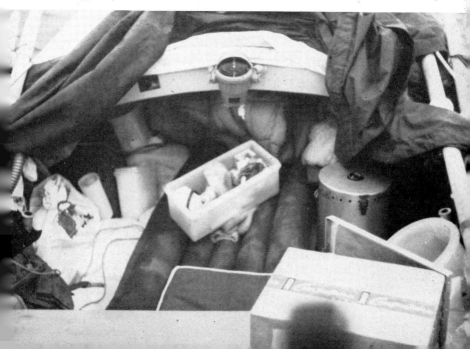

MEALTIME: *Above left* Setting up the cooking stove

Above Cooking—the stove and pressure cooker had a specially-built shield

Left Enjoying my favourite meal—curry

Lonely as I was, sharks were companions I could have done without

A close-up of Bluey

Hansa—a very cheering sight and the last of the three ships that gave me positions

Drying clothes was always a problem—particularly after *Silver* overturned

when describing in detail the sort of hazards I would have to face. I now knew that nobody could picture in words exactly what lay in store out in the Atlantic. It had to be seen. I had seen it and there was a lot more to be seen.

I was quite a sight too. My beard was matted with dried salt water, my eyes were red-rimmed and sore and my face felt as raw as a piece of beef. Salt sores had begun to erupt at the corners of my mouth. A rash of them had begun to build up on my neck, wrists, armpits and, most uncomfortable of all, my backside.

Wherever salt water had managed to penetrate between skin and clothing—and that was everywhere—it had crystallised and had rubbed and chafed away at the skin with every movement I made. And every movement made them burn, as if acid were being slowly but regularly dropped into the heart of each individual sore.

I looked lousy and I felt lousy. But my luck of the last few days was still holding good right into the morning of 5 June. The temperature climbed to 48°F. That, after what I had been through, was virtually a heat-wave. Near midday the sun actually poked a way through that grey lining overhead.

The clouds split apart, showing a large patch of blue, blue sky. And the sun, blazing, almost blinding, poured its healing warmth into every aching bone, every smarting sore and every throbbing bruise on my body. Hurriedly I stripped off every stitch of clothing and sat there stark naked, arms outstretched, head flung back and for a few minutes slowly turned from left to right and back again, trying to make sure every inch of skin, including my still blue-looking feet, got its quota of that life-giving warmth.

The water in the kettle was still warmish from my morning tea. There was about a pint of it. Using it with care, I bathed and washed until most of the salt crystals disappeared from my skin. A change into clean clothing and I felt like a new man.

Then I spread out on the seat, basically the only really dry spot on *Silver*, and basked in the sunlight. The wind was from the west and light. Perfect rowing conditions. I should have been bending my back, not sunbathing. I would, however, have defied anyone to resist the temptation to lie in that sun.

F

The lazy, luxurious warmth drove home the truth of how truly lucky I had been to survive the Labrador Current.

For the first time I begrudgingly admitted to myself that there had been times when I wondered if I would ever make it. As soon as the admission was made I forced it out of my mind with all the will-power at my command. To admit that was to admit the possibility of defeat and I was convinced that once I allowed even the slightest doubt to shadow my mind my resolve would weaken and it could be the first step towards failure.

Failure? Just failure? That sounded no more than giving up rowing and just walking ashore somewhere. Like a boat on the Serpentine which heads for the boathouse when its hour is up. Out there in the Atlantic an honest man has to face up to the inescapable fact that failure means one thing only . . . death. And that I could face up to. It would be no disgrace to die so long as I had fought every inch of the way.

I closed my eyes to shut out the sun's brightness. I was amazed, and pleased, to discover that I could so calmly think of death. I had never thought of it before, not even in the Borneo jungle. There, of course, I had had companions to share the hardships, to joke at the discomforts and to dismiss any spot of trouble, no matter how severe, as just part of a normal way of life.

I suppose I must have half dozed off there in the sun. The thought of my friends brought them all very close. In a sort of fitful half-dream I saw them all as plain as life. They were all there—'The Horse', Nick, 'Lofty'—all grinning, all shouting. They were buzzing round *Silver* in rubber Gemini assault craft. They came aboard and each man carried a two-dozen crate of beer.

Strange how little *Silver* could take so much extra weight without apparently showing any ill-effects. In my dream even as I was lifting a bottle of beer to my mouth I puzzled about it. It wasn't natural. I can remember looking over each side of *Silver* to make sure she was okay. She was riding perfectly. I stopped puzzling. But as I took my last look over the side I suddenly spotted that the Gemini craft had drifted away. They were bobbing away, drifting further and further from *Silver*.

Puzzlement turned to panic. All my effort so far had been for nothing. Instead of making my landing, having rowed the Atlantic alone, I would be stepping ashore with a crowd of chums. The whole adventure would be a non-event. I would have to start all over again, back to St Johns, back through that Labrador Current. I groaned at the thought, 'Oh my God . . .'

Suddenly I was cold again. My body began shaking—and I was wide awake to find myself blissfully alone. That grey blanket overhead had knitted together again, blotting out the sun. A glance at my watch showed that it had lasted between twenty minutes and half an hour. I shook my head, grinned at the memory of my dream and looked around at the customary greyness.

The wind was still light and from the west. There was nothing to do except get out the oars. I kept *Silver*'s stern to the wind and maintained a steady rowing action. Under these conditions one has to fight off the temptation to pull like mad. It would serve very little purpose. I would be exhausted in a couple of hours and in no condition to cope with any change of wind which threatened to short-change me on any progress I made.

My inexperience had already tempted me into that sort of error earlier in the trip. Now I knew better. In any case, I figured that I must conserve my strength. Every day, every hour in the Atlantic must, to some small degree, eat away at my reserves of energy. I had to guard against any reckless use of my powers of endurance.

Once again my Army training was to come in useful. Strange how so much of a soldier's training can be adapted to survival at sea. I had learned how to doze while stepping it out on a forced march when a certain amount of distance had to be covered in a certain time no matter if you had not slept properly for days. I suppose that this 'marching doze' was really a state of mind. A situation where one could shut off about twenty-five per cent of one's active self, mentally and physically, and yet automatically keep putting one foot in front of the other. The closest comparison I can think of is that old line which used to appear in tales of the Wild West: 'a Redskin sleeps with one eye open'.

I found that I could comfortably adapt myself to doing much the same while rowing. The oars dipped in and out, I bent backward and forward and it became as automatic as placing one foot in front of the other. I am sure that this cat-napping while on the move helped tremendously to conserve my strength which would otherwise have probably been frittered away in bouts of huge physical effort.

But the cat-napping brought with it an attendant danger: mental indifference. I had been warned about it. I knew it would happen. I knew it was happening to me then. With the few days of quieter weather, the blissful peacefulness of a calm ocean and the cosiness of a gradually increasing temperature, part of my mind had slowly, almost imperceptibly, become dulled and lethargic.

I noted with surprise how much slower my reactions had become. Yet, at first, I did nothing to counteract the danger. It was almost as if I had somehow managed to step outside of myself and observe my body taking part in a weird slow-motion film which had no ending. The hours must have slipped away and yet I had no sense of speed or time. Nothing at all seemed to matter any more.

That was the danger sign and luckily I managed to recognise it in time. I knew if I ever got to the stage when I failed to spot the danger signals then I, *Silver*, the entire adventure, was heading for disaster sooner or later.

Silver rocked gently in the westerly breeze, lulling me deeper and deeper into my waking sleep. I struggled to whip my mind into a state of activity. It was a strange and eerie process. Telling myself I must find something to do, I would look slowly round *Silver* trying to decide what it should be. Before I ever hit on anything the reason for looking had been forgotten and once again I would have to flog myself into mental awareness.

It was impossible to judge just how long I dithered about in this half-conscious state. It seemed to last for days and yet I was aware that I continued to row. Just how effective my rowing was I will never know. I have a deep suspicion that it was basically nothing more than lifting the oars in and out without bothering too much about pulling, steering or even reading the compass. I am sure of one thing. It was too long. Half an hour in that fuddled state would have been too long.

I think the break-out was successfully reached when I began to compare my condition to that legendary but dubious character of old colonial days, 'the white man who goes native'. That led me to thinking of the traditional Englishman who, even in the darkest jungle, always dresses for dinner. I used to laugh at that idea. There was no laughter this time.

I rested on my oars as I grappled my way to the conclusion, a devastating realisation in my state of mind that dressing for dinner was nothing more than a form of self-discipline. And wise discipline imposed by oneself, or by anybody else, never did anybody any harm.

The struggle of grappling with so many successive thoughts almost proved too much. I had reached the state where I told myself that no matter what I thought one thing I couldn't do was slip into a dinner jacket and bow tie. I was about to give up again, and quite willingly, when I realised I was tugging fiercely at my scruffy weeks-old beard. Maybe I couldn't dress, but I could shave. And I would shave. I did shave with hot water, scented shaving soap and a brand-new blade.

It worked. I was jerked out of my mental muddle, but I have never been able to decide whether it was the actual act of shaving or the agony of scraping a blade across weatherbeaten skin and salt sores which opened up until the blood ran down in a dozen rivulets. I preferred to think it was the act of shaving.

By the time I had staunched the flow of blood on my face it was 11 am on Friday, 6 June. I could only vaguely recall creeping into my shelter to sleep, but I could not be absolutely certain that my memory was not of the night before. I had drifted through nearly twenty-four hours without knowing much about it. And I didn't like it.

The temperature had dropped again. It was down to 44°F. I remembered the sunbathing of yesterday morning. It had been a wonderful 48°F before that sun broke through. And the temperature had obviously risen above that while the sun shone. For a wild moment I feared that *Silver* had drifted back towards the icy clutches of the Labrador. That savage stretch of current would prey on my mind until I was so far away from it I knew that it would be impossible to return.

Flicking a glance at the still-leaden sky, I wondered if the sun would break through again. Then perversely hoped it would not. I blamed that lulling warmth of yesterday for accelerating the dangerous state of mental indifference into which I glided. The wind, still from the west and dead astern, had dropped to between 5 and 10 mph. *Silver* was steady and heading due east. She was nipping along beautifully.

A few days ago this would have been the perfect situation to lure me into dropping all thought of doing anything else except row. Admittedly I could have pushed her speed up a little by getting the oars out, but while she was heading in the right direction there was a far more important chore to do. I checked the lashings on the rudder and slightly adjusted them to keep *Silver*'s bow pointing east and then re-tightened them.

With that out of the way I set about sorting out *Silver*'s trim. At that point there was not actually anything to worry about. She was sitting nicely in the water. But I had used eight gallons of drinking water. In terms of water supplies this was nothing to worry about . . . a mere half-gallon a day was a rough average of the rate of usage. But it meant four empty spaces which had each been filled with two-gallon plastic containers of water. Each one a vital factor in maintaining *Silver* on an even keel. Those containers had to be filled with sea water, the caps marked to distinguish them from the drinking water and then replaced beneath the floorboards.

All my water supplies were stowed away in this fashion and thus acted as ballast for *Silver*. I was not taking any chances on upsetting the little dory's balance. For I had been told that the two journalists who drowned when their rowing boat *Puffin* overturned during an Atlantic attempt had overlooked this precaution.

I think these few days were probably some of the easiest I spent in the Atlantic. And it was just as well. For though nothing went wrong while I was handling the water containers, I was well aware that I was doing everything at a very much slower speed than was normal for me. The effects of 'mental indifference' were taking longer to wear off than I thought. But at least I was able to congratulate myself on the fact that, despite the slowness, at least my mind was able to beam in on whatever I was doing and remain concentrated on that without wandering or forgetting.

But by Sunday morning, 8 June, I had something else to keep my mind occupied. The wind still light, still no more than 15 mph, had swung right round until it was hitting me from due south. Luckily it was not too strong to row. From 5 am until 8.30 am I rowed to the north-east, trying desperately to conserve as much of my hard-earned ground as possible. I judged that I had made fairly good headway and, deciding not to wear myself out, I heaved out the sea anchor while I breakfasted and read my Sunday letter.

It was from Major Woods, the unit's education officer. By sheer chance I had picked the very letter which would set my brain ticking over, help to get it speeded up a little. I may not have anyone to talk things over with, but these letters helped, in the most magnificent way possible, to bridge the gap of loneliness at the very point when one might get a sense of desperation for the sound of another human's voice.

Major Woods's letter set me thinking, all right. He wrote of the force of motivation; of the will to go on no matter what lay ahead; of the need to believe in oneself and of why so many start but few succeed. He emphasised that one must be 100 per cent positive, not a whisker less, then luck and good fortune—if any at all is coming your way—will carry you the rest of the way. I figured that I had been 100 per cent positive and that I had been getting quite a fair share of luck. All that remained was for that state of affairs to last.

Folding the letter and replacing it in the plastic box, I told myself it would last. As I looked up, I saw the evidence of my luck all around me. A mist was rolling in. Thick and white it curled around *Silver* until I could only just see her bow. The beautiful, wonderful, delightful Arctic Smoke. The surefire visible evidence that I was leaving the waters of the Labrador Current and sailing into the warm embrace of the Gulf Stream.

6 | Lost and found
9-16 June

The silence was uncanny. It came rolling in with the fog, dissipating the wind and flattening the water. *Silver* and I were trapped in a cell of dripping condensation. Huge glistening drops settled everywhere like quivering blobs of quicksilver as the dory softly tilted on the gentle swell.

Curling fingers of mist undulated around me as I tried in vain to see further than fifteen yards. Clammy, dense and impenetrable, it lay over the surface of the sea and literally ruled the waves. There was not a whisper of wind to disturb it and I looked in wonder over the side of *Silver* at the suddenly still waters, calm, black and glassy. And the silence! The incredible experience of not hearing a sound except that of my own breathing came almost as a shock after days of having my ears filled with the roar of the sea and the screaming wind.

After a breakfast of hot porridge and instant coffee I unshipped the oars. If ever there had been a true chance to row this was it. *Silver* slid through the mist, setting up a steady hissing sound and spreading ripples across the black glassy water. As time passed by I became obsessed with the notion that there may be a ship close by. Unseen, unheard, lurking in the fog, just waiting to smash *Silver* to splinters.

I started counting my strokes and at every twenty I would stop rowing to listen and look. Cupping my right ear with my right hand I turned my head slowly, sweeping the area on the starboard side of *Silver* from stem to stern. Then changing hands and ears I would do the same on the port side. Not a sound. Rather idiotically I had overlooked taking basic precautions as soon as that fog surrounded me. I had failed to test the miniature fog-horn bolted to my shelter roof alongside the compass and I had not hoisted my metal radar reflector on the radio mast. Shipping the oars, I did not waste any more time putting those ordinary safety measures into operation.

When I had tested the klaxon back in the carpenters' hut at the SAS camp it had sounded strident enough to be heard clear across the ocean. In that muffling fog it seemed to be no more than a rusty squeak. It sounded so pathetic I just sat down and laughed. I reckoned I could shout louder than that. And to prove it I cupped my hands round my mouth and bellowed: 'Ahoy there! Atlantic row-boat *Super Silver* here and bound for Blighty.'

The resonance of my own voice bouncing around on the foggy walls surrounding me both startled and delighted me. It was almost as good as having company. So good, in fact, I shouted it out several times, pitching my voice at differing levels just to see what effect the fog would have. Then I hoisted the radar reflector. There was no more I could do to protect myself except trust that if a ship did cross my path it would be equipped with radar and an operator alert enough to pick up the infinitesimal speck of light that my reflector would throw on his screen.

The fog stuck with me through the day. By mid-afternoon there were no signs of its dispersing and I began to worry about the night. Should I chance sleeping? Or should I sit up all night listening for the sounds of imminent danger—a bell, a fog-horn, the throb of slowly turning engines?

I plumped for sleep. I had seen so few ships it was hardly likely that one should run into me just because it was foggy. In any case, I had originally planned always to sleep whenever the weather allowed me to do so. A blunder made in an emergency because of lack of sleep could prove every bit as fatal as a crash in the fog. It was a case of six of one and half a dozen of the other as far as I was concerned. And having made up my mind I stopped worrying about it.

At nightfall there was still no sign of a lift in the fog. But I rowed on for a couple of hours, determined to grab as many miles as possible. It was like moving through a ball of black cotton wool. When I crawled into my sleeping bag it was a few minutes after 10 pm. I think I was fast asleep within seconds.

It was a huge shuddering bump, shaking every timber in *Silver*, which woke me. I jerked upright and shot out of my shelter so fast I forgot all about first getting clear of the sleeping bag. It slithered to my ankles, trapped my forward step and laid me in a breathless heap across the seat. As I lay there trying to kick my way out of the bag and wondering what the hell had happened, something rumbled and rasped down the full length of *Silver*'s port side.

Finally kicking off that clinging bag, I scrambled to my feet to turn my head rapidly in all directions, straining to pierce the ball of black cotton wool in which we were still wrapped. There was nothing to be seen, nothing to be heard: no lights, no bells, no sound of ship's engines.

'Then what the hell was it?' I asked myself aloud. 'A floating log? A large piece of driftwood? An empty oil drum? Some ungainly piece of flotsam from a ship?'

Had *Silver* been damaged? Was she leaking? Even as I was rattling the questions at myself, I dived back into the shelter grabbed my flashlight and examined every inch of *Silver* inboard from end to end and side to side. Not a sign of damage. Not a scratch.

My sigh of relief was cut off almost as soon as it started when another fear gripped me. Had *Silver* been damaged below the water-line? On all fours I crouched to shine the flashlight over the floorboards, at least as much of them as were not covered with my supplies. There was no sign of water flooding in. I hoisted the little trapdoor which led to the compartment beneath the boards where my fresh-water supplies were stored. Once again there was nothing to raise alarm.

And yet I could not turn off my concern. Maybe *Silver* had not been holed, but suppose, just suppose, she had been weakened by that thump just below the water-line? How long would she hold out? How long before the pressure of the sea, especially in rough weather, forced its way through the weakness and flooded *Silver*?

Those unanswerable questions nagged and tormented me. There was only one thing I could do. I would have to go over the side and find out for myself. And it had to be then. I did not dare wait for daylight. For the morning might bring winds, making the sea far too rough for me to risk taking a dip. I stripped off in the pitch blackness of that foggy night, leaving only the plastic-bag protection on my still numb feet. A lifeline was strapped round my waist and the free end lashed to the after samson post, and over I went.

I gasped for breath as I ducked my head beneath the cold, glassy surface. The underside of *Silver* loomed green and ghostly in the light of my waterproof flashlight. Strings of sea grass which had collected on her hull snaked out in the current, sliding across my hands, arms and face. Slowly, painstakingly, I worked my way along the entire port side, prodding with my fingers, gently stroking with my hands, feeling for the tell tale crack or dangerous splinters. Then I repeated the performance along her starboard side. Again not a scratch as far as I could find.

My delight at finding *Silver* as sound as a bell knew no bounds. I hauled myself inboard, teeth chattering, limbs trembling, but grinning with sheer joy. I towelled myself down until my skin tingled with the rush of blood through my veins. Once I had dressed and changed socks and plastic bags—I had to keep my feet dry—I made a massive cup of cocoa and sat there drinking it and giving *Silver* the odd loving pat and telling her: 'You are a real beauty.' If I had grown fond of that little dory during this trip I had now fallen in love with her.

It was difficult trying to get to sleep again. I lay there staring out into the darkness with my eyes wide open and thought: 'It's great to be alive.' And I prayed. It was a prayer of thanks, really. I think the previous day's Sunday radio service from St Johns had left quite a mark on me. I had actually listened and enjoyed it. I marvelled at the thought of myself actually wanting to listen to a church service. What a fantastic change!

As a youngster at Fegan's Homes in Stony Stratford, Buckinghamshire, I had to go to church three times every Sunday. I hated it. I grinned in the dark as my mind went drifting back over the years. They used to give us sevenpence or eightpence a week pocket-money, depending on our age, every Saturday, a penny of which went on sweets bought at the home's tuck shop. How we used to scramble round that sweet counter! I wouldn't want to criticise the food at the home. It was no doubt wholesome and plentiful. But there were not many of us who enjoyed it.

It all seemed years and years and years ago. And as my eyes closed at last, I remember thinking, with some pride, 'No matter what I thought of Fegan's at the time, it didn't do me any harm.' In fact I was cocky enough to feel that they had not done too bad a job on me at all.

By morning the fog had cleared. That unplanned dip in the Atlantic must have knocked some of the stuffing out of me. I slept until gone 9 am. I figured it must have been more like a bout of unconsciousness than a night's sleep. The wind from due south had swept away the ghostly mists and was building up steadily. By ten o'clock it was howling in at gale force.

Silver was being driven north and once again I was helpless to do anything about it. I threw out the sea anchor and hoped we would not drift too far off course. But I needn't have been so gloomy. For the next five days the winds were generally from the west and never above 25 mph. The temperature dropped below 50°F only once, and then by only one degree, and once it actually soared to 60°F.

That was a fabulous day of sunshine; the day I first wore a straw hat purchased in St Johns when I, very sensibly I thought at the time, felt I ought to have some protection from the fierce sun which would no doubt be beating down on my head for days on end. I didn't have to wear that hat again for the rest of the trip.

And all the time I was eating up valuable milage to the east. I suppose I should have been feeling chuffed under such almost perfect conditions. I even got my rowing organised on a fairly civilised basis of three hours on and one off. I should have sensed nearing home with every stroke, yet those days dragged by, long, slow ponderous hours.

At first I could not fathom what was wrong with me. I supposed it was just generally a feeling of anticlimax after the sustained punishment from the Atlantic. And that is what I had to keep telling myself, for the truth was not too long in dawning.

It was simple. I was pretty crocked. Groggy, punch-drunk, call it what you will. I realised I was feeling absolutely battered. I ached all over, as if I had taken a thorough pounding in a rugby match which had been played non-stop for several days.

It was no longer the ache of stiffened muscles which could be ironed out with a session on the oars. This was deep-seated pain. Putting it simply, I reckon I must have been bruised from head to toe. And now it was beginning to tell on me. Now I was beginning to learn the deeper meaning of endurance. And endure it I would, even if I had to row with one hand.

To talk myself into taking things easy while I had the chance would have been too simple. The temptation to lie down for a few hours in the belief—a mistaken belief, I am sure—that I would be resting myself was fairly strong. Just how long is a few hours? My suspicion was that a few hours would almost certainly stretch into yet another few hours, perhaps even a couple of days, if the weather lasted that long, hours or days which would be utterly wasted. There was absolutely no doubt in my mind that the temptation had to be resisted.

In a deliberate attempt to be methodical I jotted down on paper a plan of action. I mapped out a programme that would keep me steadily busy. Perhaps the most important was working out my new rowing schedule of three hours on and one off. In those off-duty hours, apart from mealtimes, I slotted a number of items all of which had a vital bearing, if not immediate at least in the future, on my safety and the success of the trip.

For example, I had been eating mostly from the supplies stowed at the stern. This had naturally resulted in *Silver* settling her bows deeper in the water as the days passed by. Admittedly, at that stage, we were not in any sense facing imminent danger, but I knew it would not be wise to allow the margin of risk to widen any further.

To my delight I discovered that, despite my low-ebb physical condition, my brain was ticking over sharply enough. For even as I was thinking of *Silver*'s trim it struck me that I had been unable to check the condition of her rudder since setting out. And it would obviously be sensible to check the rudder while it was just a little higher in the water. Trimming *Silver* would be the second job.

I had determined not to rush things; to pace myself and just take everything as steadily as possible. I could not have rushed the rudder inspection even if I had wanted to do so. I had to climb on to the top of my shelter and then, lying as flat on my stomach as possible, slide over to one side of the five-foot stretch of turtle decking which covered the after buoyancy compartment. Being absolutely smooth, the turtle decking had nothing to offer in the way of handgrips.

I managed to hang on by wrapping the fingers of my left hand over the edge of the bow and hooking my left foot round the wooden samson post set between the turtle decking and the shelter roof. I slid my right foot over the edge of *Silver*'s other side and pressed inwards with both feet, just as a horseman grips the flanks of his mount. The plastic bags on my feet made it difficult to maintain a firm grip, but luckily *Silver* was fairly steady and I managed the job in reasonable comfort. My lack of height, of course, helped considerably. A taller man would never have been able to flatten himself as I did.

From that spreadeagled position I had a pretty good view of the rudder. Apart from sea grass, which was beginning to gather on the lower half, it was in perfect condition. The eye-bolt hinges showed no signs of weakening and there were no signs of strain on the wood. Laboriously I slid backwards to the roof of my shelter, crouched there for a few seconds to regain my breath and then set about sprawling myself out again in order to examine the other side of the rudder. That too was okay.

Back in my cockpit I broke open a can of beer—my fourth at that stage of the trip—and downed it in almost one gulp. Another can would have been more than welcome, but, although I had another thirty-two cans on board, I decided against a second drink. My plan was to save them for the hot weather which I was so sure was due to come my way before too long. As things turned out, I could have drunk the lot then and there, for there was to be no blazing summer for me.

The rudder inspection had taken up nearly three-quarters of my non-rowing hour. I sat on the seat for the last fifteen minutes mentally sorting out where the stores would be redistributed when I set about re-trimming *Silver*. That job also took up nearly the entire hour. It was not so much a matter of the amount of work involved, for I had only to shift twenty-four days' provisions from forward to aft. It was the extreme care with which I had to ensure that each item was stowed away in exactly the right position. I felt that I just could not risk even the slightest list to either side.

I clucked away at this job like a fussy old broody hen. After moving two or three packages I would squat as low as I could to measure up, as far as possible, the alignment of *Silver*'s bows with an imaginary line in the sky. Then I would raise myself until my eyes were on a level with the horizon and try to line up the bows with that. As a third check I stood on the seat with legs fairly well spread apart in an attempt to 'feel' if *Silver* was level or not.

It occurred to me at the time that I was probably being over-elaborate with my precautions. But not being an experienced sailor I could not leave it all to instinct. In any case, the concern shown for *Silver*'s trim by those hardy seafarers back in St Johns had indelibly impressed itself on my mind.

Perhaps the most cheering point of all was that my pro-gramme was working out so well. Slowly the list of ticks against the items I had pencilled down grew and nothing went wrong.

Even my plans for an emergency water supply came through with flying colours. During a hard downpour of rain one night I spread out a rubberised canvas poncho—Army issue—be-tween the gunwales of *Silver*. When the rain stopped I found that about two and a half gallons had been trapped in the poncho. I was overjoyed at the efficiency of this makeshift gadget. I filled up one of my empty two-gallon water containers and poured the rest into my spare kettles and pressure cooker. Even if I had to stay in the Atlantic longer than I anticipated, at least I would not run out of drinking water too quickly.

12 June, bringing with it my one day of summer and a tem-perature of 60°F, marked the last of the easy-going days of light westerly winds. Not knowing the weather was due to change the next day, I decided to make the most of the sun. I altered my rowing schedule to two hours on and two off. It also gave me a chance to pay a little attention to my feet. Off came the plastic bags and socks. I rolled my jeans up as far as possible and stuck my feet into the sunshine.

They were still swollen, too swollen to wear my sea-boots.

Although I had tried to ignore them, they had been causing me more anxiety than I cared to admit. They certainly did not seem to be improving rapidly enough for my liking. It alarmed me a little when I discovered that I could not really feel the sun on them. I was, however, convinced that the sun would be good for them. There was one consolation: they had started stinging a couple of days back. The blood must have begun running through them once again. And now they were stinging like blazes. There was nothing more I could do, so I told myself: 'They'll be okay in the end,' and tried to forget them. In any case, on a day like this, there were plenty of other things to think about, to remember.

Having looked at, and dismissed, my feet and lolled back in the sun, it was a fairly natural switch to think of my favourite way of spending a summer's weekend—a twenty-mile walk through the countryside. It would have been great to have been able to step over the side of *Silver* and head straight for the hills and a cosy country pub at the end of the walk. My mind uneasily turned once again to my feet. I wondered if they would ever be fit enough to take me again on a walk like that.

Moody and angry that I had allowed myself to slip into another bout of worry, I forced myself to stand up. I grabbed every bit of damp clothing I had and spread it out to dry. It was laid over the seat, over the shelter roof—anywhere, in fact, where the sun could get at it. *Silver* looked like a floating laundry.

Feeling a bit better at last, I chuckled as I thought how handy it would have been to have a woman around the boat for this sort of chore. Naturally she would have to be pretty and shapely. I checked over all the girls I knew and wondered if any woman would accompany a man on a trip like this. I didn't think so, somehow. It just went to prove that old feminine belief that women are far more practical than men.

I reminded myself that there was nobody back home so deeply attached to me that they would worry unduly. So why the hell was I worrying about myself? My feet could drop off, just so long as I managed to do what I had set out to achieve— get *Silver* to the other side of the Atlantic.

But to do that, I told myself, I would have to impose a rigid system of self-discipline. I have never regarded myself as a particularly brave person. Certainly no braver than the next. Courage cannot be weighed, balanced or measured. It cannot be doled out to those who need it or taken from those who have an excess. It cannot be switched on and off as and when needed. One does not even know if one possesses it in enough quantity, or even any at all.

Self-discipline is the only way I know of dealing with difficult situations, whether they are mental or physical. It is, if you like, a substitute for courage. And a damned good one at that. But only if you are prepared to be your own martinet. And, like everything else, discipline is something you have to learn. I learned all about it at Fegan's home. Up at 7 am, stand by your beds, wash, inspection for cleanliness, then prayers and a breakfast of porridge and doorsteps of bread and margarine. After that we were packed off to school in the town and were back in Fegan's by about 5 pm. Once again the routine of wash and cleanliness inspection before tea.

We were a pretty rough bunch of kids at Fegan's. Every day somebody would be on correction duties. This sort of punishment would be inflicted for a number of reasons: fighting, swearing, stealing, dirtiness or lack of punctuality. I had a full share in them all. The correction duties usually amounted to something like cleaning drains or scrubbing floors for a couple of hours. I didn't like it at the time. I hated it. In fact, if anybody had told me then that it was all for my own good I would have spat in his face. But they would have been right. I have never had any reason to regret anything that happened at Fegan's.

Having given myself that little lecture, I set about living up to my own beliefs. What, I asked myself, had I neglected most during the trip? What needed instant, positive action? The questions were merely an exercise. I knew the answer. Navigation had been so sadly neglected it had been virtually non-existent. I had relied practically entirely on getting the compass needle to point east as often as wind and weather would permit.

That I had been heading generally in the right direction there was no doubt. But where was I exactly? Was I too far north or too far south? I guessed, and it was mainly guesswork,

G

that I was a little further north than I would have liked. The last, and only, fix given to me by the Portuguese skipper of the *Rio Alfusqueiro* was no longer of any real use in trying to estimate my position.

I had to face it. Basically I was lost. If weather and drift carried me too far to the north there was every chance I could miss the Irish coast altogether, Scotland too, perhaps, and then be swept on up to the icy waters of the Greenland and Barents Seas. I found myself searching the waters ahead of *Silver*; looking far, far ahead. Looking for what? It was almost as if I was hoping to see a signpost or a policeman of whom I could ask the way.

Some fish which had been following me all day were still alongside *Silver*. Small, grey shapes just a few inches below the surface, sometimes almost motionless except for a flick of their tails, then darting forwards or sideways in a flurry of action to gulp down, no doubt, some tasty morsel which I could not even see. They looked happy enough. At least they knew where they were. And if they didn't then they were certainly not worried about it.

I had hoped to be able to use the plotting board I had used in the Army to work out my fixed-line position. But that should have been used every day to be of any use, and that had been absolutely impossible. A plotting-board route depends on being able to draw straight lines and accurate angles. It was okay in the classroom back at camp, but not here. I grinned ruefully at the thought of trying to draw straight lines in the roaring weather *Silver* had been through.

Yet there was a way if I did not have to wait too long. I figured that I could not have drifted far enough to take me right off roughly the same latitude as Greenwich. That could be used to advantage. My nautical almanac would give me the time of sun-up at Greenwich. All I had to do was wait for an unclouded sun-up out here, then divide by four, the difference between the two times to find the degrees west of Greenwich. This is accurate to within fifteen miles. Maybe it would not suit the *Queen Elizabeth II*, but it would be more than good enough for me. All I had to do was wait for the first clear unclouded morning.

Friday, 13 June, lived up to the old legend as far as luck was concerned. The dawn was as grey as slate and there was no change in that situation throughout the day. There was no chance to try out my system for making a fix. The wind, too, decided it had neglected me too long. Not only was it building up in strength, but it was coming from the north. The previous night a ship had passed about a half-mile from me. Quite obviously it had not spotted me. Now, I felt sad that I had not put my half-thought into action, to fire a flare to attract her attention. Then I could have asked for my position.

I had been so sure that the sun would shine for at least a second day, and I had also suffered a miserly urge to conserve my flares for real emergencies rather than fritter them away, that I just watched the ship sail out of sight. But there was no time for wishful thinking. By the afternoon *Silver* was shipping quite a lot of water. My cosy days were over.

That afternoon was a comedy of minor irritations. As I was sitting down to a late lunch, a freak wave broke right over me, filling my pressure cooker and ruining the curry. I made do with a tin of fruit. Then I discovered that the water was not draining through the floorboards quickly enough to get to the suction outlets of the pumps. With axe and sheath knife I hacked a hole roughly three inches by three inches in the boards to help it on its way. Rough and ready maybe, but it worked.

And just to pile on the agony I found my chronometer had been flooded and the batteries ruined. Some of the spare batteries for my transistor radio had also been made useless by the sea. I anxiously examined my deep-sea diver's wrist-watch, but that, at least, was still going strong.

The next three days passed at a sort of plodding pace. I can hardly remember them at all. The entries in my log are mainly confined to wind and temperature. I think the rowing and my bruised body were really getting through to me at last. One entry for 14 June certainly seems to indicate that I was in a pretty hazy state. It simply reads: 'Gas cooker blew up.'

It is impossible to recall exactly what happened, but I am sure that I turned it on and then found the matches were damp. Foolishly I left the gas running while I hunted for more matches. One touch of the lighted match and a sudden blaze of gas singed my eyebrows and the backs of my hands. Luckily there were no burns. I think I was so soaked with sea water by that time that nothing short of a forest fire would have made any impression on me.

The days passed in snatches of memory. I remember wishing that I'd kept a count of how many hours' rowing I had done each day. And I remember thinking how perverse this business of rowing turned out to be. Sometimes it drives you mad with pain. Sometimes you don't notice it at all, it becomes almost automatic. What an astonishing amount of useless trivia the memory bank does store up!

The only interesting item was a St Johns radio programme commemorating the fiftieth anniversary of the first trans-atlantic flight by Alcock and Brown. I remember the announcer saying that they took sixteen hours twelve minutes and my telling myself: 'The next time I want to cross this bloody ocean it will be by bloody plane.'

Finally the danger signals hammered through my thick head. I needed sleep and to hell with my bright ideas of keeping busy. I had overdone the self-discipline bit. Thankfully I crawled into my sleeping bag. Then, after swallowing a large shot of rum, I was deep in the land of zizz. I slept almost solidly for a little more than twelve hours. The only disturbance was a sort of instinctive clock that made me wake three times just to check that all was okay, and that I did without getting out of the sleeping bag.

I woke just before dawn on Monday, 16 June and was, by com-parison with the last three days, a completely new man. It was about 5.45 when I woke. I sat up breathing in the air and watching the lightening sky. Oh glory be! What a wonderful morning. The sky was blue and getting bluer by the minute. At last I would be able to put my makeshift navigation system to work.

With the aid of my nautical almanac I went to work on my little mathematical problem. It was a perfect sun-up at 6.22 by Greenwich time. My calculations put me at Latitude 48°N; Longitude 38°W. I made that 840 miles in a straight line east of St Johns. I reckoned that I had actually covered something like 1,200 miles in all. But whichever way I worked it out it meant I was coming up to the halfway mark.

One thing I did know then. Nobody can really come through this adventure alone. Sometimes I almost thought God was in the boat with me.

7 | To hell and back
17-20 June

Sea birds, black-headed, grey, white and yellow-beaked, hovered just a few feet above me. Their outstretched wings braced and slightly quivering as they thrust their snowy chests into the wind. Dipping, soaring, banking, they effortlessly kept pace with *Silver* with no more than an occasional flutter of their wings. They had been around for several days. *Silver*'s turtle decking and some of the stores bore the evidence. It was decorated with seemingly well-aimed drops of lime.

I would shake my head with mock anger and dare them to aim at me. Every now and then one would dip his head sideways and a single beady black eye would fix me with a knowing stare.

They were my only companions and I was glad to have them. It seemed as if the birds had accepted me into the exclusive circle of strange beings who made the Atlantic their home. And I was honoured. I saved food scraps and fed them each day. There was a never-fading fascination in watching the extraordinary grace of those long sudden swoops to the water, finishing up with the most expert dip of the beak to scoop up the scraps before they sank too low for recovery.

I tried to tempt them closer by placing scraps on *Silver*'s turtle decking. It was days before one of them overcame his suspicions enough to risk landing there. He came fluttering in to perch himself on the very tip of *Silver*'s stem as far from me as possible. His arrival was the signal for an outbreak of harsh cawing cries from his companions still circling overhead. It was as if he had been ordered in as some sort of advance patrol and was now being asked for an immediate report. He squawked just once and there was silence from above.

I am sure every bird there was watching his every move as he perched there on the stem, head flicking left and right and his body continually bobbing as if ready for instant take-off at the slightest alarm. But at first he did not move towards the food.

Sitting stock still, I scarcely dared to breathe for fear of scaring him away. After a few moments the bird took two or three hoppity steps towards the food, stretching his neck full length and recoiling in short bursts of reconnaissance. Then he stopped and, with a lightning twist of his head, flashed an un-winking wary eye at me. A few more jerky steps forward, an-other stop and then he would inch forward again.

As soon as he had started to move that had been the signal for a continuous and strident outcry from his friends in the air. It was for all the world as if they were trying to divert my attention away from that little drama on *Silver*'s forward turtle decking.

Finally that straining beak closed over a delectable middle cut of a two-day-old sardine. At that identical moment the raider, with a flourish of wings, was back in the air, almost giving a victory roll as he swooped upwards to accept the screeching plaudits of his envious chums. Before long one or two of the braver—I preferred to think of them as friendlier—birds were eating regularly from that turtle-deck café. I watched them and nurtured our friendship with great care. It was not difficult to believe that those stories of long-term prisoners making pets of rats in their cells had more than a ring of truth about them.

Isolation, exposure and hardship play havoc with a man's proud supposition that he can face anything alone. I had been at sea one month and spoken only to the crew of the Portuguese trawler *Rio Alfusqueiro*, to *Silver* and to the birds—and sometimes to myself.

Yearning for the sound of a human voice, I tuned in the radio to St Johns. They were broadcasting a documentary-type pro-gramme about the Battle of Waterloo. The fact that stuck in my mind was that the Duke of Wellington's bounty for that battle had been £60,000 compared to £1 6s 8d for a private soldier. But they had nothing to say about the private soldier who, at that moment, was figuring that a chat with the birds was bounty enough in his personal battle with the Atlantic. There was, of course, no reason why I should have been mentioned.

I hadn't been sighted for something like three weeks and therefore I just wasn't 'news'. Yet not to hear my name mentioned made me a little sad. It was extraordinary how I listened to news broadcasts hoping to hear something about myself. I wondered if I wanted to hear it so that, in a funny sort of way, I could reassure myself that I really was okay and heading for home. Months later I was to discover that although I did not figure in many news items, some people, both in the United Kingdom and in Newfoundland, feared the worst.

Yet, though there were times when I felt a little dispirited, I am sure that at no time did I ever think I would not get through . . . at least, I never allowed myself to think of failure. Some people may look upon it as childish, but I had, and still have, great faith in that old saying: 'There is no such word as can't.' But to prove it you have to fight. And I was going to have to fight that night as never before. I was to discover that the horrors which had gone before were but a taste of the terror which was to come.

At eleven-thirty on the night of Tuesday, 17 June, I was still comfortably coasting along in a steady 15 mph westerly. I had been rowing steadily and was more than happy with the day's progress. As I shipped the oars the blade of the port-side oar was awkwardly struck by a wave while it was balanced precariously on the gunwale and, of course, out of the rowlock. The oar spun out of my hand, slid rapidly over *Silver*'s side and disappeared into the darkness. It was, of course, sheer carelessness on my part. I should have made sure the oar was hoisted well clear of the water and balanced in such a way that if I did lose my grip, then it would have slid inboard instead of out.

An extremely minor mishap, for I had five oars left, but I kicked myself for slackening my guard in that way. For those spare oars were not there so that I could gaily fling the odd one overboard. They were there to guard against the possibility of broken oars. And every oar could be vitally needed.

I was in a foul temper and practically grinding my teeth with rage as I turned in for the night. Something like two hours later I had a bumper crisis on my hands. The lost oar was completely forgotten.

Silver was tossing and turning, bucketing and shuddering in a gale that came screeching out of the night. The wind was 50, 60, perhaps 70 mph. There was no time to try gauging it accurately. It didn't matter. We were getting our worst battering of the trip, that I knew. In the darkness the rushing waves looked like skyscrapers and water was pouring into *Silver*.

I had found, some time before, that when alone in moments of stress and anxiety such as this it helped to shout orders at myself, and as I grabbed for the pumps I was shouting: 'The pumps, you fool, get to the bloody pumps.' Looking back now I think that this business of ordering myself about gave me such a sense of urgency that I was under the impression that I was moving and reacting faster than normal. And that impression was very comforting.

Silver was being thrown around so much that it was absolutely no use trying to kneel at the pumps or even lie down between them. I had to jam myself in there with the aid of my folded life-raft and the stores and then pump, pump and bloody well pump again. There was no let-up at all. The pumping sessions lasted throughout the night and into the next day while the wind tried to blow *Silver* from the face of the Atlantic.

I didn't kid myself that night. I was literally fighting for my life and I knew it. There were moments when I thought *Silver* would be pounded to kindling wood; moments when the sudden lift of a wave shot *Silver* up and up into the night, leaving my stomach several feet below me, while I wondered if I was going to be thrown out of the boat.

This was the fifth storm I had had to ride and I shall always, in retrospect, marvel at the secret strength of that little Yorkshire-built dory. Wave after wave thumped into it with teeth-rattling impact. I would not have been the least surprised if it had shaken apart, board by board, around me as I lay there.

When trying to describe the anger and the hunger of the sea there always seems to be the danger of being over-dramatic. Yet the fact is that a turbulent ocean is stark high drama. Such ferocity unleashed over such a wide area for so long a time crushes a mere man back to size—puny, helpless and crazy to think that he could defy such mighty power. Looking back, the issue was a simple one. I was going to either live or die.

That night, however, I swear there was no time to think of

living or dying. There was no time to allow fear to wind its sticky fingers around my heart. In short, the Atlantic can be so frightening that to be afraid would mean the game was up.

The incredible savagery of movement, wind, water and noise tots up to a degree of violence which could balance the mind on the edge of insanity. It batters the body, dazes the brain, drains the lungs and assaults the ears for hour upon hour until it seems there is no escape, that it will never end. Once that thought is allowed to take root I am sure it is the moment of doom. And if, by fluke, death does not arrive, then the Atlantic has a gibbering fool at its mercy.

I don't think there is anybody who can truly advise how to live through that sort of torment alone in a storm-tossed flimsy shell of wood. I can only offer what I think I did.

Seas breaking over *Silver* constantly flooded my nose, eyes, and mouth, which fell open more often than not to suck in vital breath. With hands almost constantly at the pumps there was no opportunity to use towel or handkerchief. In any case they would have been sopping within seconds. But I gained spasmodic momentary relief by spitting to clear the mouth and snorting and blowing to clear the nostrils.

As far as my eyes were concerned, the easiest thing was to keep them closed most of the time. And by shutting out the sight of the fury around me I built a barrier against fear. In some extraordinary way I was able to close my mind to danger; to ignore the excessive cruelty of this cruel, cruel sea. All that is left to do after that is to hang on until you either sink or survive.

I found myself blinking at vicious streaks of dawn when trying to shake some of the water from my eyes. Streaks of sullen dirty yellow which changed shape and size constantly as low-lying clouds of black malice charged across the sky, hurrying to wreak their malevolence on whom and whatever they could find. And still *Silver* was being twisted, thumped and shaken until the sky seemed to be rocking and twirling to such an extent that I was sure the entire world was about to turn turtle. I would not have been surprised if I had suddenly found *Silver* and myself riding through the clouds and looking down at the ocean.

The fury lasted through the morning. I could not eat. I could not even pause for a cup of tea. It would not have been possible to boil a kettle even if I had dared to leave the pumps.

At noon the nightmare of a storm began to run out of steam. At first slowly, then with a suddenness that was uncanny, the wind dropped and faded to a 10 mph caress. The waves fell away as if weary and snuggling down to rest. I stared in wonder at this instant peace and continued to pump until *Silver* was clear. I felt as if I had been to hell and back.

The clouds were now a puggy white and behind them the yellow haze of a hidden sun tried to dry them up. This diffused sunshine glistened on the still wet floorboards of *Silver*. Strewn all over the boards and tucked in between the stores was the debris of the storm. Bits of seaweed, an odd shell, grains of sand, a couple of jellified creatures and a strange little pink fish no longer than three inches. The fish was dead, but I threw it back, along with the weeds and jellies, as if I could appease the Atlantic by returning its lost property.

Yet I could not shake off the thought that this calm was nothing more than the Atlantic having a fit of sulks while it worked out a new plan to get at the property it really wanted: me and *Silver*.

Luckily I was so hungry I had little time to brood. A curry was soon bubbling away in my pressure cooker. As I lifted the lid I sniffed at that life-giving aroma like a Bisto Kid in seventh heaven. Beer, sardines and biscuits and cheese rounded off the meal. But I was still hungry. A tin of fruit and two spoonfuls of honey stopped the gap. Then I permitted myself the luxury of a shot of rum.

I rolled the liquor around my tongue, swilling it from one cheek to the other until the inside of my mouth was stinging. Then I swallowed it, trying to jolt it into the pit of my stomach in the hope that the impact would fire me with new life. I took another drink in the same way and gradually the fumes began to rise, pricking the back of my nostrils and seeping into my head. I was slightly tipsy and it felt good. The rum did its work well.

After two hours' sleep I decided to get some rowing done. The wind had remained steady at between 10 and 15 mph and was still from the west. It had been from the west all night. That had been the only consolation. *Silver*'s head was pointing due east as she slid along on her homeward course. To me it was the sound of music.

As if to cheer me and make sure I was still okay, shoals of flying fish appeared, throwing themselves through the air for a few feet before flopping back into the sea. There were about a couple of hundred of them, never more than a few feet from the boat. I had heard that they made a great fried delicacy. None landed on *Silver*. In truth, I am sure that if they had I would have thrown them back. After the previous night I felt that everything had a right to live for as long as possible.

But I was not to be left in peace for long. By late evening the dread wind, still from the west, thank God, began building up its new fury. And the frenzy began all over again. For two days it blew. Never falling below about 30 mph and reaching into the seventies in the wild bursts of angry temper. I had thought that I had got used to Atlantic weather. I was wrong. I would *never* get used to it. There were times during those forty-eight hours when I thought I could actually hear the prayers of my friends back home. I prayed. And it does not stretch my imagination to think that God heard me. For I am still alive. And while I live I shall never forget those terrible days.

By the morning of Friday, 20 June, I was in a mess. My hands were so sore from the continual pumping duty, and the joints so stiff, that they stayed cupped as if still round the pump handles. Blisters had been giving me constant trouble. Because my hands had been wet for three days the skin of dead blisters peeled off and then yet another blister formed as I got cracking at the pumps. In between the really heavy winds I managed to smear them with Lanolin and Vaseline. Maybe it was imagination, but it seemed to ease them quite a bit. In any case, I had to ignore the pain, for I dare not stop pumping.

My old salt sores itched like mad and the new ones burned as if cigarette ends were being stubbed out on my skin. After cat-napping at the pumps for two days and two nights I felt as if I was going to drop off wherever I happened to be standing, sitting or crouching. And I felt so filthy I would have given a week's pay for a hot bath.

While clearing up, I found that my thermometer had been broken sometime during the monumental storm. The last reading had shown a temperature of 54°F. Not overwarm, but at least there was the satisfaction of knowing the danger of freezing was long gone. But I was in no condition to worry overmuch about anything less than an emergency. As the winds had lessened to no more than 30 mph for the last couple of hours, I decided to chance taking a much needed nap.

I woke three hours later at about 11 am. Weather conditions were roughly unchanged except that now it was a little foggy. I thought it must be low cloud, for it was more than a thick drizzle. Visibility was down to between 250 and 300 yards.

Making a rough calculation of my position I reckoned I should be nearing 30° West. That would be about halfway. It was a depressing thought, for during my preparations for the trip I had figured that this would be the hardest part of the whole journey.

All the signs had been that if anything was going to go wrong mentally with me then it would happen roughly between the point I had now reached and just past halfway. I was actually pretty sure that due to my experience in the Labrador Current I had already struggled through that dangerous mental stage. But I could not be sure. It was just something more to stop worrying about until it caught up with me.

Although I was by no means convinced that I was as near to the halfway stage as my rough plotting had indicated, I decided to prepare for it. For at that stage I would be coming within range of the RAF Shackletons on their Atlantic patrols. I checked over my Sabre radio with great care, for the thought of having a chat with someone was overwhelmingly cheering.

I would be able to ask them to pass on a message to the folks back home. Perhaps the newspapers would be interested enough to run a small story. I wondered what sort of headline I would write if I was sitting in a newspaper office when the news came in.

'Moby McClean safe.'

Not very bright, perhaps, but, to me, being safe was the most important thing in my life right then. The thought of getting a message through to the outside world drove me once again to try the two-way radio on the off-chance of picking up a ship. I had tried about half a dozen times since I left St Johns but had not had any success. This time, I hoped, would be lucky.

Out went my hopeful message, searching for a friendly ear. 'Atlantic row-boat *Super Silver* calling. This is Moby McClean . . . come in, please.'

But it was no go. There couldn't have been a ship within range of the radio and its full scope was 200 miles. There was nobody at all at any point within a radius of 200 miles all around *Silver*. How lonely can you get? I must admit it was a somewhat depressing thought. But there was nothing I could do about it—except shrug and tell myself: 'Oh, you'll get used to it. Don't forget, the first six months are the worst.'

8 | The loneliest battle
21-29 June

I had been lost for hours in the pages of one of the three books I had brought with me. The pages were swollen and warped from the damp, but were still readable. *Sailing to Freedom* is about a Finnish family who escaped when the Russians invaded Finland during the last war. It is an account of their journey to the United States in an old sailing boat. They were at sea for 130 days.

Reading of the dangers they faced and survived helped me to forget those which surrounded me. It was, I suppose, sheer escapism, although, at the time, I regarded it more as a type of shock treatment—like getting straight back on to a horse which has just thrown you. The effect on me was tremendous. My determination to succeed was strengthened: my feeling that I would not fail was deepened by the simple formula of telling myself: 'If they could do it, so can I.' I was, if necessary, prepared to stay at sea for more than 130 days, no matter what happened.

Although my food supplies had in no way been damaged, and, all things being equal, would last another sixty to seventy days, I had been taking no chances. Whatever I did not eat from each day's ration pack had been stowed away in plastic bags ready for a rainy day. For days I had been tucking the stuff away like a squirrel hoarding its winter nuts. And I had got to the stage where I couldn't bear to dump anything eatable overboard. If I had to stay out here for anything like 130 days even a few stale crumbs would be valuable.

At 5 pm the moan of a ship's fog-horn interrupted my reading. I looked up and heard it again away to the west. There was nothing to be seen. The fog of the morning was still with me, writhing and swirling, covering the sea in a cloak of secrecy. The horn sounded again and again, bellowing through the thick walls of mist. I became so frustrated with continually

trying to see through the fog that at one time I was momentarily convinced that a plane was circling overhead.

But that sound was closing on me and just could not be
coming from anything but a ship. I became very excited at the
thought that other humans were nearby. And my attempts to
pierce the fog became quite frantic. The very thought that they
might slide past, unseen and unspoken to, was utterly unbearable. I even shouted a couple of time: 'I'm over here, over
here.' Yet even as I opened my mouth I knew it was useless. So
I just stood there, leaning on *Silver*'s gunwale, staring and straining to see through the dank curtain which was cutting me off
from my fellow men.

I stood like that for a little over half an hour as the ship drew
closer. Suddenly I spotted her just 300 yards away looking like a
huge monster feeling its way through the murk. The thrill of
wild excitement which ran through me was suddenly chilled by
the realisation that they would probably never spot me in this
half-light.

She was heading straight for me. Excitement fled, leaving only
an aching anxiety in the pit of my stomach. I was sure she was
going to hit me. The very human companionship which I had
been craving would prove my end. Like a child hoping for a
miracle, I wished myself alone once again.

Slowly the monster edged towards me. My radar reflector
was not rigged up. Yet again, despite all my good intentions,
I had been caught unprepared. As I tried desperately to think
of some way of alerting those aboard the approaching ship, I
still found time to feel an unsettling flash of concern about my
mental condition. Was I slowing down? How much slower
would I get? How many more chances would the Atlantic give
me?

As the alarm signals clattered through my brain I was trying
to hoist the radar reflector into place. But it was impossible.
The palms of my hands had become studded with nothing but
stiff and stunted thumbs. Finally I compromised by holding
part of the reflector above my head in the wild hope that it
might work. I was trying to put a spot of my old jungle training
into effect. They had always dinned into us that it was shape,
shine, silhouette and movement which catches the eye. I turned

the reflector above my head and waved it slowly from side to side hoping that would do the trick. But I did not catch the eye of anyone on that ship.

I felt utterly trapped. The sea anchor was out and I knew I could never get it inboard before the ship hit me. And it was absolutely impossible to row while that anchor was out. I just stood there looking for a way out; trying to get my mind churning over; trying to think of something—anything.

The only thought I came up with was 'to get the hell out of it'. The thought of deserting *Silver* made me as miserable as sin. It was like planning to leave a friend to the enemy. I dragged out my inflatable life-raft and stood ready to snap the seal which would automatically blow it into shape. A few more seconds, I thought, and it would be over the side.

Then my incredible stupidity dawned on me like a kick in the pants. The flares! Why had I not thought of the flares? 'What a fool! What an abysmal idiot I am!' Even as I cursed myself and reached for the flares, the ship changed course and passed me between 150 to 200 yards off my starboard side.

As she disappeared in the fog, her blasted horn still sounding its terrifying warning, I realised I was trembling all over. It was not from fear. I was literally shaking with anger at myself. I had allowed myself to drift into a state of mental lethargy which had nearly killed me. And all the time I had been kidding myself that I was okay. That no matter how tired, how bruised my physical condition, I was at least mentally alert. But when the crunch came I had turned out to be a hopeless idiot of a failure.

This was what I had feared and had tried to guard against. I crawled into my dog kennel to try to forget it. I sat there, my arms circled tightly round my knees and my head pressed down hard, trying to control my shaking body. And, more important, fighting to dominate a brain which had become dulled into a dangerous liability.

I had been sitting there a few minutes when I heard that fog-horn once again growing nearer. 'Oh my God!' I thought, 'not again.' I grabbed some flares and scrambled out of my shelter. Somebody must have seen me, after all. She was about 200 yards off my stern and heading towards me at a creeping

H

pace. And I could see people along the rails waving and shouting at me.

The ship crept closer and closer until she was no more than twenty or thirty yards away. Her bows loomed high above me and I was able to make out the name *Regina Oldendorff* before she edged along until I was staring up at the bridge. She was a West German freighter and as she had closed I had heard someone shouting: 'What you want? What you want?'

'My position please,' I bawled back. But they did not seem to understand. I waved my chart above my head and then overlapped my arms to make an X to indicate that I wanted a fix. My sign language worked. By the time the bridge was abeam of me a dozen shouts had told me: '49°45′ N, 26°05′ W.' The halfway stage was not too far away, after all.

From the bridge the German captain shouted through a battery-powered megaphone: 'Are you all right?' With tongue in cheek I told him I was in perfect shape. While other people were watching I found it quite easy to put on a bold front, even though I knew how abject I would feel once they had gone.

The captain shrugged, waved and turned away to get his ship under way again. As that huge steel wall of riveted plates slid past, the crew on the rails continued to wave and shout. I could not understand them, but one word stood out like a beacon: '*Glück.*' I have since found out it is German for luck. There were to be times when I wondered if I had completely run out of luck. But I didn't need to understand the language to understand their meaning. I waved back with gratitude and the *Regina Oldendorff*, slowly gathering speed, steamed off into the fog. I listened to her fog-horn until she was out of hearing range and I was alone again.

I slept all night Nine solid hours without waking once and 21 June dawned clear if not bright. The fog had cleared and a cosy 20 mph wind from the west had *Silver*'s bows pointing happily for home.

Thinking back on the trip it is difficult for me to put into words how hard this part of the journey became. Physically I had taken a battering but was pretty sure I could take a lot more. It was the slowing up of my mental processes which worried me. I had suspected it for some time. The incident with the *Regina Oldendorff* confirmed my suspicions.

For a week the winds remained light enough to save me great discomfort but not strong enough to constantly engage my mind. I had to force myself into a rigidly applied routine; to do certain things at certain times; to whip my sluggish brain back into a state of active readiness.

In a way that fright over the *Regina Oldendorff* coming at me from out of the fog had been a fortunate scare. More important, it had been an object lesson in what I had to face. The true danger of this mental weariness is that although you know it is eating away at you it can still catch you off-guard. I did not intend that to happen again. But it did. Luckily, it was not important to my safety, but it was vital as yet another reminder that all could be lost in just a few seconds of slack thinking.

One morning I had draped my sleeping bag over the roof of my shelter in an effort to dry it out, then promptly forgot all about it until just before dusk. It had gone. I had failed to tie it down and had failed to keep an eye on it during the day.

Fortunately—I had to wonder just how many more lucky chances I would be allowed—it must have fallen overboard just a few minutes before I looked for it, for there it was floating in the water about fifty yards astern. I rowed over to pick it up, wondering how I was going to drill this brain of mine into precise activity once again.

I had already set myself a routine of rising between 5.30 and 6 am, rinsing my face with sea water and then checking over every corner of *Silver*. Then I would deliberately make breakfast last at least twenty minutes to force myself to maintain a keen watch on the time.

After that it was row. Not the sort of rowing which had mostly been the pattern before, where I rowed for the sake of rowing. This time I would row for exactly one hour by my watch, then carefully ship the oars inboard and spend exactly ten minutes going through deep-breathing and knee-bending exercises. The latter had been necessitated by the fact that the cramped space of *Silver* had at last got through to my knees and thighs. They had stiffened into a state of creakiness which could almost be heard as I moved.

Then it was back to the rowing for another hour, followed by ten minutes checking the stores and counting the number of days' rations I had left. One afternoon I arrived at three different totals. But that didn't matter, at least I had carried out the counting routine at the right time.

Row again for two hours and break for lunch, which, I had decided, should last exactly half an hour. For one hour again, then stop to count the food stocks again, but this time for fifteen minutes. And so on until 6 to 6.30 pm, when I forced myself to stop rowing for the day. The evening was similarly broken up with periods for eating, a cup of tea, writing my log, etc., and then head down by 11 pm at the latest.

At the beginning I was not concerned with how well I performed all these self-set tasks. My main object was the time-keeping. I wanted everything to run on the dot—like clock-work, in fact. I felt that if I could discipline my mind to follow and accept such a rigid time-table it would prevent it from drifting off into a sort of never-never land. It was not easy at first. I found myself forgetting to look at my watch for time-checks and consequently would quite often overrun the laid-down time.

On other occasions I found myself wanting to alter the time-table to suit my mood of the moment. For example, when the deadline to stop rowing came along I would tell myself it wouldn't matter if I kept on for a bit. In fact I would benefit from it by stretching a few more miles towards home. A couple of times, when I was scheduled to count the food stocks again, I almost did not bother, having thought, in a fuddled sort of way, that it had already been done.

They were strange days, passing by in a sort of weird slow-motion style, and I found that although it had been comparatively easy to plan the time-table, it was entirely another matter to carry it out. Perhaps the most uncomfortable sensation of all was knowing what I wanted to do and yet, at the same time, knowing that part of me was doing its darnedest not to co-operate.

It was a peculiar struggle, but I stuck at it and gradually got on top. Towards the end of the week the most I was out on any one of my timed periods was a couple of minutes. Such success almost prompted me into accepting that as a victory. The temptation to tell myself that I had the situation well under control and to relax was almost suffocating. Indeed, it was so strong that for nearly a full day I allowed the time schedule to go by the board. But I snapped to the danger just in time and forced myself to apply it with even more rigid discipline than before.

At one point I even tried estimating the number of rowing strokes I made in a day. I got to 23,000 and packed it in. My mind started positively boggling when I started trying to work out an estimated total for the trip. It had been a bad idea and I dropped it. As a way of breaking the monotony that had, far from relaxing me, left me quite tense. Over tea that evening I hit on what turned out to be the perfect answer. It was so simple I kicked myself for not thinking of it before.

My food supply counts had left me with the undeniable information that I had enough food for another hundred days, so unless something really drastic happened I was not going to starve for a long time. But I decided I had been wrongly using my tea and sugar supplies. I had been making a pint of tea at a go. This meant I could have only three brews a day and more often than not I would be drinking at least half of it when it had turned cold. From then on I made half-pint brews, thus giving me six tea-breaks during the day and I adjusted my time-table accordingly. I also decided to step up my daily vitamin intake from two to four pills a day.

Maybe it was purely psychological, but by the end of the week I was as sharp as I would ever be on my time-table. And my slow and ponderous brain was once again beginning to prod me into action at more or less the right time, place and speed. I doubt if anybody would have called me a ball of fire, but at least I was beginning to smoulder.

It was during those last few days of the week that I hit on a solution to a problem which had been bothering me for some time, but which I kept shelving because I could not think of an answer. I had forgotten to bring a can of oil with me. It was needed for many things—squeaky rowlock sleeves, squeaky rudder pivots and to protect *Silver*'s metal fittings against the corrosive rust of the Atlantic. The answer had been staring me

in the face for days: use the surplus oil from my daily can of
sardines. It worked well and I began storing it in an empty
honey jar. I even had a wild idea of using it to 'pour on troubled
waters'. Wild maybe, but that idea was a sign to me that at least
I was at long last trying to think ahead.

It was like coming to after a bout of drifting in and out of
consciousness. For the first time in the last six days I was fully
aware of what day it was: Thursday, 26 June. I had groped my
way through those days in a mental fog. Part of that time I
could remember, for the notes were right there in my log. The
rest would be a mystery for ever. I was by no means 100 per
cent mentally alert yet, but I had improved enough for the true
dangers of the past few days to come crowding in on me and
to be able to consider them calmly.

How close to giving in had that incident with the *Regina
Oldendorff* driven me? I would never know the answer exactly.
One hazard, however, was crystal clear. It was possible to stand
on the very edge of failure entirely against my will. I was convinced that my self-imposed time-table had a lot to do with
bringing me round and I determined that it would be continued whenever possible. Storms created their own time-
tables. It was another long bout of fairly calm weather that I
had to guard against.

Ah! the treachery of this Atlantic has no limits. Even when
at peace it is waiting to grab you. Day and night chase each
other until the sheer automatic monotony creates a state of
hypnosis in a wearied brain which has been working overtime
to spur on an exhausted body. And just how much had days on
end of bitter loneliness to do with such a mental state? It is impossible to make any sort of accurate measurement. I can only
explain how it affected me at times.

One night during the past week I had spotted the lights of a
ship winking at me from far away in the east. An overwhelming
desire to attract attention, to talk, to shout, to wave and to
delay that ship for as long as possible almost tempted me into
using my flares. The luxury of human companionship became
as vital as breath itself. I forced, literally forced, myself to turn
back on those lights and to check the illuminated hands of my
wrist-watch for a full fifteen minutes. When I turned again the

lights had gone. There was nothing but the velvety, choking, empty Atlantic night. A great wave of sadness, as if I had lost a best friend, washed over me until I felt I would drown in it.

I had added to my time-table a fixed routine of listening to the morning and evening news broadcast every day. I had just started to pick up the BBC. My idea was to switch on at the exact moment of the start of the broadcast and to switch off at the end. My object was to instil some discipline in myself and, no matter how much I may want to hear a music programme, I must follow my own orders to the letter.

On the evening of Wednesday 25 June I switched on as usual. I heard the programme introduced and then a couple of loud crackles came from the transistor set and then silence. I juggled with the knobs, I shook the set, I changed the batteries, I tapped it, I hoisted the telescopic aerial and pushed it down again several times.

The set was dead. I sat looking at it hardly able to believe what had happened and absolutely unable to believe such bloody awful luck. I think it was the most depressing moment of the trip. A sense of utter loneliness pressed in on me until I felt as if I had been cut off from the rest of the world for ever.

Emotions of this type are, of course, momentary, but they seem to last for hours, with the added risk of being plunged into a pool of self-pity which I consider to be one of the biggest pitfalls in this sort of adventure. I had to break this feeling of being sorry for myself. I needed a sense of competition, I thought, to occupy my mind. As the idea occurred to me, the name of John Fairfax popped up like a jack-in-the-box. That was the man I had sworn to hate; the man I had sworn to beat . . . oh, how long ago was that? It didn't matter how long ago. A good hate session against Fairfax would put me in a good competitive mood.

He must, I figured, have made land by now. That should have been enough to get a good head of hate going. Somehow it didn't seem enough. I switched to a mixture of envy and hate. Fairfax, I told myself, is right now wallowing in hot baths, comfortable beds, long pints of cool beer and probably has a beautiful girl sitting by his side. It still didn't work. It made me envious all right, but I had no hate left. 'Good luck to him,' I told myself. 'My turn is coming.' I was to discover a few weeks later that Fairfax himself had still been at sea at the time.

But I did have a friend out there waiting to encourage me with a few words. I found him on Sunday, 29 June. He was right there in my Sunday letter. It was from my old regimental sergeant-major. The best way to illustrate the amount of comfort I drew from that letter at that particular time is simply to repeat it.

The address he used for himself was: 'From where *you* are trying to get back to . . . and *will*.'

He wrote: 'Just a few pearls of wisdom from one who has never rowed more than 100 yards. No doubt you will become depressed. But when you talk to *Silver* it is *not* a sign that you are going off your head but that you are coming to terms with the boat and the sea.

'You are never really alone. All sailors, from the dawn of time, have found it easy to speak to *God* when they felt the need for guidance. At times, when you are afraid, remember He is quite near. So give Him a good old shout and He will answer by helping to calm your fears.'

9 | Sharkbait
30 June-5 July

On Monday, 30 June, I reluctantly wrote in my log thirteen words that I hated to read: 'I must confess that, at last, I am beginning to feel worn down.' To even admit it was like wringing a confession by torture from me. But the facts had to be faced and, if possible, dealt with.

The winds were still light. Little more than breezes, in fact. But for the last three days they had been switching back and forth like a yo-yo. Northerly one day, south the next and that morning I had woken to a south-easterly. Not to be able to proceed in the one vital direction had become sheer frustration. I knew I must have passed the halfway mark and yet I could not convince myself that I had.

My mental condition was still patchy and, although I stuck to my time-table like a drowning man clutching at a straw, it was difficult to shake off the tormenting idea that I was actually heading back to Newfoundland. I actually began wondering whether or not I should consider seeking help if things became too bad. If things got to that pitch I would have to ask for aid from the next ship I spotted or call up assistance on the radio. But judging from the number of ships I had seen it could be days or weeks before another came along.

As *Silver* slid through the grey waters I totted up the for-and-against scorecard. The side for giving up totted up in rapid-fire style. I had been at continuous full stretch now for just on six weeks. Every muscle, every nerve, every sinew and every tiny brain cell had been strained without let-up with the single object of keeping myself alive. I was a mass of aches, bruises, blisters, salt sores and a couple of agonising boils had begun to erupt on the back of my neck. I was filthy and itchy to such a degree that I felt as scabrous as a mangy cat.

The rowing was becoming more difficult, and sleep, even during these calm nights, was transformed into fitful restlessness.

And I was going off my food. The only thing I really fancied the last two or three days was canned fruit.

And the salt! The ever-present salt. I was caked with the stuff. Practically everything in the boat was covered in a thin white crust. It was in my hair, my nose, my eyes, under my clothes and I could not get rid of the taste.

That was the case for giving up. I had to ask myself, could it get worse? The only answer was not only that it could, but would. But if I decided to surrender what could I do about it? The answer was just as obvious. Nothing.

That was the case against giving up. That and the fact that despite my discomfort there was still a little voice inside me telling me I was not beaten yet. I had to be sure that I could hang on and would. I wondered, if it were possible to be granted just one wish, what would I ask for? I decided that right then it would be a pair of braces. My oilskin trousers kept slipping down in Chaplinesque style because the elastic waistband had perished. I had tried tying them up with a piece of string, but it did not work at all well.

Not a very imaginative wish, perhaps. Even a little crazy. But it served to help me resist wishing for the impossible—the feel of land under my feet. But my feet were not yet really ready for the land. Although by this time I was able to pull my sea-boots over a couple of pairs of socks, they were still too tight. The swelling had decreased until my feet looked almost normal size once again. But that was about the only normal thing about them. They still had that pickled look and they were still stinging and painful. They were, however, quite obviously on the mend and that was all that mattered.

The hours slipped by, virtually uncounted and unheeded. They merely acted as markers for my vital time-table which I hoped would help me nurse my mind and body back to strength.

On Tuesday I managed to work out a rough position. I made it 50°30′ N, 28°43′ W. Maybe it was not pinpoint accurate, but it must have been as near as possible under the circumstances. I was over the halfway mark at last and truly on the home run. There could be no thought of giving up now.

Looking back on that moment I now realise, with some surprise, that the discovery that I was over the halfway mark caused very little excitement. If it had happened a week or ten days before I would have felt like throwing a party. My elation would have known no bounds and it would have been a moment of congratulations to both *Silver* and myself.

I had been looking forward to that moment ever since I left St Johns. It had been the big goal, the massive target which had kept me going through the most severe experience of my life. Yet when it came it brought only a slight sense of relief. I am only thankful that it was enough to bolster my determination with the sort of cynical resignation used by most servicemen to describe the early period of their careers: 'Cheer up! The first three years are the worst!'

It was without cynicism, however, that I recalled reading, some time ago, the prayer of a sailor's mother. I believe it was written in the Victorian age, but I cannot remember the author's name. It ran:

> O Heaven, my child in mercy spare!
> O God, where'er he be;
> O God, my God, in pity spare
> My boy tonight at sea!

How corny that verse sounds now. How real it sounded halfway across the Atlantic. Under those conditions the strongest heart, I feel, would wonder if it was to be spared.

It has been said that sharks, like vultures, can sense the dying and travel many miles to attend the feast at the wake. I think it must be true. At 2 pm on Wednesday 2 July I saw my first shark. It slid alongside silently and without warning. I was emptying my after-lunch tea leaves over the side when I saw the sinister grey shape keeping pace with *Silver*. I knew there were sharks in the Atlantic. I had, of course, expected to see them. But this first meeting was so sudden I nearly dropped my tea-mug over the side. He was so close, I swear I could have reached over and touched him.

Once I had got over the shock of his sudden appearance I watched him for a few minutes swimming alongside and all I could think of at first was: 'My God, but he looks bloody ominous.'

I looked round on all sides of *Silver*, expecting to see triangular fins cutting through the water. God knows what I really expected to see, but in that first wild moment I thought the sea would be littered with them and all heading for *Silver* like U-boats zooming in for the kill. To my surprise, and great relief, there was not another shark to be seen.

One shark, however, was more than enough for me. This one kept me company for seven hours. First he would appear on one side of *Silver*, then on the other. At times he would disappear from view for five or ten minutes, but then suddenly swim back into sight again. He swam alongside *Silver*, ahead, astern and underneath. There were times when he came so close that I could hear him scraping the boat.

When he first appeared on the scene I sensed a chill of apprehension such as I had never quite felt before. And it did not begin to wear off until at least an hour had passed. I suppose that one can get used to practically anything in time, even a shark.

What, I asked myself, does one do about a shark which appears bent on much more than just a passing acquaintance-ship? I tried chucking old tins over the side, hoping he might choke on them. Like a true gourmet he completely ignored them, disdaining even to honour them with a sniff. Should I, perhaps, try throwing so much food over the side that he would eventually become so full that he would swim away and forget me as a possible delicacy? I had no idea, however, how much food it would take to fill a shark and, in any case, I was going to need it myself.

Hours later, it seemed, it dawned on me that I couldn't possibly feed every shark that came along. It annoyed me to find that my mind was still churning over in such a ponderous manner. That shark had shaken me more than I had thought possible. But I had nothing else to do. The winds were still light and I figured that trying to think of ways to get rid of my unwanted companion was as good mental exercise as anything else.

Wild ideas, some just plain stupid, were examined with care

and gone through step by step. It did not matter how unworkable they were so long as they kept me thinking.

I toyed with the notion of making a hook out of one of the rowlocks, baiting it with a paste of biscuits and porridge cake and trying to catch the blighter. The fact that I didn't even have a file with which to fashion the hook did not stop me working out the best way of shaping a rowlock for the purpose. I even went to the extent of planning how to shape it into a barbed hook.

I planned an ambush. The basis of this was to tempt him close to *Silver*'s side with titbits and then to spear him with one of the oars after fashioning the shaft end into a point with my clasp knife. At one stage, recalling a Tarzan film I had once seen in which Lex Barker had wrestled with an alligator before stabbing it to death, I flamboyantly thought of jumping over the side and tackling him with my knife. Needless to say, I didn't bother to work that one out. The only logical conclusion was that one day *Silver* would be found empty and drifting.

Finally I ran out of ideas. The last one was to give the shark a name. At least it would make the situation seem a little more chummy. I dubbed him 'Bluey'. Nevertheless, I was glad to see the last of him at about 9 pm. He sped off to the west and I watched him until his fin was out of sight. I heaved a sigh and said: 'Cheerio, Bluey, don't bother to call again.'

But he did. Bluey showed up again the next day. At least, I assumed it was the same shark. He slid on to the scene just as before, silent and sinister. It was about midday and I had been rowing for several hours. I don't know how long he had been keeping an eye on me, but as I was shipping the oars to prepare my lunch I spotted him about two yards off *Silver*'s port side and just about a foot beneath the water, grey, vicious and apparently ravenously hungry. And again he kept pace as *Silver* drifted before a 15 to 20 mph wind. I scanned the water to see if he had brought any of his friends along this time, but again he was alone. Maybe he figured I was big enough only for a meal for one. I watched him nosing along as I ate, not too heartily I must admit, my curry lunch.

With a pathetic spot of bravado I waved my spoon at him and said: 'That's right, Bluey, just hang around until you

think I'm fattened enough for your liking.' Even as I spoke
I shuddered as my imagination vividly presented me with a
picture of Bluey grabbing me by an arm with his jaws. I knew
I was brooding far too much on Bluey. If I went on like that I
really would begin believing that I was about to end up as
sharkbait. In an effort to forget him I tested my lifeline radio.

As I had not yet succeeded in picking up a ship's operator,
I made my call without too much enthusiasm. Almost mechani-
cally I mouthed my little message: 'Atlantic row-boat *Super
Silver* here. Come in, please.'

I had repeated it several times when I heard a faint voice:
'Sailing ship fifty miles to your north.'

Almost jumping with excitement, I shouted at the top of my
voice: 'Hello, hello there. Atlantic row-boat *Super Silver* here.
Come in, please.'

Again that faint voice. And again the same message: 'Sailing
ship fifty miles to your north.' He repeated it several times. I
cut in with: '*Super Silver* here. Are you mistaking me for a
sailing ship? This is row-boat *Super Silver* . . . row-boat *Super
Silver*. Do you read me, please?'

He obviously did not read me, for all I heard was another
message about a sailing ship. I gave up trying to tell him differ-
ently and switched off. And when I looked over the side Bluey
was still with me. The sheer persistence of the brute was unnerving. He did not disappear until dark. Even then I could
imagine him slipping quietly alongside *Silver* and just waiting,
waiting, waiting . . . for me.

I woke on Saturday, 5 July, to a wind from the east. It built
up to forty miles an hour and, although it was from the east and
causing me to lose precious distance, I blessed it. For Bluey did
not appear. He had no doubt headed for the calm of deeper
water. The wind lasted all day and there was nothing for me to
do except heave out the sea anchor. I stayed in my shelter all
morning, trying to build up my strength. I dozed off and on
most of the day turning and twisting on the hard floorboards.

My discomfort, as I tried to rest on those boards, was a result
of the clinging inertia which had possessed me with increasing
danger over the past two weeks. My air bed was no longer in-
flated. A week before, the constant rubbing against other

articles in the shelter, as *Silver* rolled and pitched her way through the sea, had worn a hole right through the side. I had forgotten to bring a repair outfit with me. My desultory attempt to patch it with Elastoplast and Bostik lasted a few hours only. A sudden hiss of escaping air and it was as flat as a pancake within a few seconds. It had been like that ever since and I hadn't bothered to try patching it up again.

An insignificant mishap, perhaps. And certainly of no importance in terms of my safety. But it was yet another illustration of the risk, lurking like a submerged iceberg, which could rip the bottom out of my adventure simply by allowing myself to drift into a stupid state of not caring. These little incidents drummed home again and again the inescapable fact that if anything goes wrong in a lone adventure of this sort there is nobody to blame but yourself.

I had reminded myself of this before. I had to keep reminding myself. There had been moments when the temptation to lie back and say: 'Well, I've done all I can, now it is up to luck, or fate or God' had been almost unbearable. Yet I had been able to pat myself on the back and say that I had fought against that —and fought well.

By lunchtime it came to me with a knock-out impact that for the first time I had given up the fight without knowing that I had done so. I had been lying in my shelter all morning bemoaning my luck, kidding myself that I was not giving in and wallowing in self-congratulations for having fought the good fight so well. The whole morning had gone without my once remembering my time-table; without my once making the conscious effort of prodding myself into even the most ineffectual action; without my once remembering what I had to do simply to stay alive.

The dawning realisation of the chilling truth jolted me psychologically as nothing else had done so far on the trip. I was literally panting with anxiety as I scrambled out of the shelter. I tried to stand and drag in great heaving breaths of that Atlantic air to steady myself.

But I could not. Whether from the effort or shock I don't know, but my knees were trembling so much I just could not keep my feet. It was not just a quivering type of tremble.

Seized by rapid shakes which seemed to be moving my knee-caps at least two or three inches and sending shuddering jerks along the muscles of my calves and thighs, I found that my legs were completely uncontrollable.

I sat down on my rowing seat, legs outstretched as far as possible and clamped a hand over each knee. I sat there with my eyes shut, rocking slightly backward and forward until the fit of shakes died away.

One thing was crystal clear at that point. I had to get into action, and quickly. My mind, however, was not so clear. I have a distinct recollection of not wanting to move from that seat. My thinking mechanism was hampered by a haze of such improbabilities, impossibilities and wishful dreaming that I think I was like the amateur mountain climber who, having got so far, made the mistake of looking down. I just wanted to stay put. To cling on to the one spot which seemed so safe.

If I moved would I fall? If I moved would those damned knees start jerking about again? If I moved . . . if? I had to move. Slowly I opened my eyes and looked at my hands. Even more slowly I eased their grip on my knees. Nothing happened. I shook each leg in turn. Again nothing happened. The trembling had stopped. Gingerly I got to my feet, expecting the whole ghastly business to start again. It did not.

I felt as much like eating as jumping over the side, but it was the handiest thing to start. I went about my preparation for lunch in such a deliberate fashion that it was almost like moving in slow-motion. 'God almighty,' I told myself, 'if you get into a state like this again it is you who will be cooked.'

The aroma of cooking curry that day, usually so mouth-watering for me, became a repellent odour. I had been off my food for a couple of days but I never dreamt I would see the day when the smell of curry would actually make me feel sick. The more I thought about it, the more it affected me. It swirled around my head in great choking waves until I thought it would actually stick in my hair. The first spoonful produced such a bout of nausea I had to force myself to swallow it. Food was vitally important to me at that stage. I knew I had to eat that dish of curry even if it took me the rest of the day to get it down.

Without a doubt it was the worst meal of the trip. And as I sat there literally willing myself to spoon, swallow, spoon, swallow, Bluey popped up again. Mealtimes were like a magnet to him. There he was suddenly alongside *Silver* again, just a few inches below the surface with that evil fin cutting its own narrow wake in the water. In an almost mesmerised state, I sat watching him until my curry had grown cold. I started eating again, stuffing the cold mess into my mouth with haste. All I wanted to do now was finish it. And all the time I watched that shark.

Thinking that the hot bite of a dehydrated curry block might give him a bit of gyp in his belly and drive him off, I threw one over the side. He did not even give it a glance. As if to demonstrate his contempt of that feeble effort, he changed course, sliding head-on towards *Silver*'s beam. Something, his fin, back or tail, rasped along her bottom as he passed underneath to take up his shadowing position on the other side.

Then I realised that this time Bluey had not come alone. At first glance the sea around me seemed alive with those dreaded grey fins. At second glance I counted only five. *Only* five? Five or fifty-five, what did it matter? For some reason which I could not fathom, none of them approached as close as Bluey—if, indeed, it was the same shark. Maybe it was my imagination, but I was convinced that it was one and the same. I told myself I could make out marks on his body, the shape of his head, his length, etc., all of which, as far as I was concerned, made a positive identification.

'Christ,' I told myself, 'this bloody sardine is getting you down. If you don't watch out you'll be giving him a free meal— yourself.'

I had already taken photographs of him. I did that the first day he appeared. I started another snapping session then, as if to show him who had the upper hand. I snapped him from a standing position, from a sitting position, from the stern, from the bow.

To blazes with him. I was on my way home and I was going to get there, Bluey or no Bluey and with or without his companions. And, I shouted at him, 'I'll make it even if you follow me all the way.'

I

10 | A whiff of home
6-14 July

When darkness fell I tried to forget the hauntings of Bluey and his chums. I hoped that by morning they would have sheered off, leaving me once again in solitary state. There were so many things for me to consider that I desperately needed some time completely free of diversion, shock or danger.

Most important of all was, just how was I getting along? The wind had been from the east for two days. Despite the fact that I knew I had put in quite a deal of rowing in the past couple of weeks, my mental state had been so persistently patchy that I had taken no count of the hours and only a very rough check of the direction. How much ground had I lost?

Under the beam of my flashlight I had a look at the compass before turning in. Sure enough, I was heading west. Nothing during this journey has been so morale-sapping as those times when the wind has you heading willy-nilly in the wrong direction.

I groaned and then cut myself short. I had been doing too much groaning. Severely I told myself, 'That is the first step to giving up the ghost.' Giving myself a mental shake, I placed myself under two strict orders as I bedded down:

1. Snap out of the lethargy which is clogging you both mentally and physically.

2. Get *Silver* heading in the right direction and get as much distance under your belt as soon as possible.

I tried to introduce a military crispness and urgency into those orders. As I stretched my aching bones out on the hard boards of *Silver*, I kept repeating them until I dropped off into a troubled sleep. At three-o'clock in the morning a crack of thunder which seemed to have made a direct hit on *Silver* shook me wide awake. There had not been much in the way of fair weather on this trip, but this was the first thunderstorm I had run into.

There was no more sleep for me that night. The storm lasted three hours. I do not think I have ever known anything quite so fantastically fierce. *Silver* seemed to rattle with every clap of thunder. The noise from the skies filled the entire space between sea and sky, rolling and echoing in the blackness until it seemed as if some unseen monster must be hurtling towards me at breakneck speed. And in between the thunder I could hear the sea swishing and surfing as it built itself up in a fury to match the rage overhead. The wind came whistling in, developing itself—it seemed to me almost with glee—into a continuous savage scream. And it came from the east, pushing me yet further and further away from home.

Every now and then the thick, choking, booming blackness was split by great streaks of forked lightning. It cleaved its way from sky to sea in vast electric sparks like the side-effects of some monumental scientific experiment being carried out by crazed gods and going hopelessly wrong.

The lightning was perhaps the most comforting and most frightening part of the storm. Comforting because each streak lit up the sea for split seconds and it was a blessing to find even fractional relief from the blindness of the night. And frightening because each fork seemed to be working its way closer and closer to *Silver*. Each streak of power was so hostile that I felt it must surely sizzle and steam as it dug its way down into the dark waters. Little *Silver* wouldn't stand a chance if she was struck . . . just a puff of smoke and a few black ashes as our epitaph.

Silver had begun to buck and pitch with growing violence. There was something almost supernatural about that alien night as I clung to the seat and listened to the boiling savagery around me. Then the rain began. It fell in sheets from the beginning. Pouring down, drumming on *Silver*'s turtle-decking and pecking with throbbing persistence at my head and shoulders. The almost biblical-style tempest was now complete.

I was wearing two sets of waterproof clothing and I pulled both hoods tightly over my ears to cut out the noise. But there was no escape. I realised that if I sat out in the open much longer I ran the chance of becoming scared. There was only one remedy: a spot of the old ostrich treatment. I dived into my shelter and tucked myself as far up in one corner as I could get. One consoling thought I hugged to myself as I sat there in the darkness—it was 100 per cent certain that Bluey would no longer be in attendance.

I was right. By daybreak the storm had begun to fade, but the rain continued to lash down and there was not a sign of Bluey or any of his chums. I had not felt so chuffed for days. The wind had dwindled to a mere 25 mph, but it was still from the east. Monday, 7 July, was the third day on the trot of easterlies. For a moment I felt the lethargic depression of the previous day creeping in. Then I remembered my orders of the night before.

That easterly wind had to be beaten somehow. I hauled in the sea anchor and started rowing head-on to the wind. The sheer uselessness of such effort was not lost on me. But I stuck at it, driven on by the perverse fit of cussedness which I hoped to make a substitute for the spirit of lethargy. I rowed for three hours, knowing full well that I was getting nowhere. Every time I began wondering how long the easterlies would last I chased the thought out of my mind by the simple formula of saying: 'It can't last for ever.'

By mid-afternoon I had to give up. The sea was running high again and *Silver* was shipping water in dangerous quantities. I had to stand by the pumps at least twice in every hour. But I was glad to be there. I was being forced to fight again. The pumping sessions made me realise just how much punishment I had taken. My muscles were stretched to torture point, but the pain was a blessing as it stung me into sharp awareness for the first time in over two weeks.

My concern about the easterlies was banished the next morning when I woke to a 20 mph west wind. By ten o'clock it had risen to about 40 mph and *Silver* was zipping along so beautifully in the right direction I almost cried with joy. After lunch the wind dropped, but I didn't care, it was still from the west. Feeling that I could not afford to waste even a second, I began another crushing session of rowing. I kept at it until dark without even stopping for tea.

I clawed my way through the first two hours of rowing,

ignoring the pain as my back creaked with each movement and my arms felt as if they would drop off. For most of the time my eyes were tight shut and my teeth so tightly clenched that my jaws ached. Then suddenly I was through that curtain of agony and rowing automatically, insensitive to the demands I was making on my physical strength. What was driving me? I wish I had known the answer. With almost clinical detachment I examined myself as I bent backward, forward, backward, forward, plodding on and on and not daring to stop.

One thing was clear. I was not out there striving for anyone or anything. Success or failure meant nothing to anyone else but myself. Strangely, I had to remind myself that I had decided this was the only way for me to make something of myself; to make the world notice me even if only for a short time; to make a place for the name of McClean on the lists of those who have dared and won. But however I wrapped it up there was no getting away from the fact that I was doing it for myself. For money too? I admitted that had also come into my calculations. What about pride? Yes, that even more than money.

Whichever way I looked at it, I kept coming up with the same question: 'Am I being just bloody selfish?' And there was always the same answer—'Yes, you are. But you're stuck with it now.' There was no doubt that this habit of handing out self-lectures every now and then was a real lifeline. I daresay the lads back at camp would have had a chuckle if they had known. They would have said that it was a foregone conclusion that I would talk to myself if there was nobody else around.

My worries about being delayed by easterlies completely vanished on Wednesday, 9 July. That morning marked the beginning of twelve days of westerly winds almost without a break. I didn't know it at the time, but it was really the start of the last lap.

It was also a great day for a very different reason. An examination of my feet showed that they had almost fully recovered from the rigours of the Labrador Current. Those frozen days seemed such a long way off, yet I felt that I could remember any minute of them. I resolved that never again would I go through anything like that and, as if to seal the vow, my sea-boots slipped over my feet with ease.

I stood up as excited as a child on his first visit to the circus. I stamped each foot in turn and danced a little jig of joy. Perhaps the most curious sensation was that of feeling fully dressed for the first time in weeks. It was incredible that a pair of rubber boots could create such a change in my mood.

The rash of salt sores on my neck, wrists and backside showed no signs of lessening. The blisters on my hands still built up one on another. My muscles ached so much that if I moved to relieve the pain in one point it cropped up somewhere else. The boils on the back of my neck felt like mountains. And trying to sleep had become a nightmare. My shoulders had started to give me so much pain at night that it was impossible to lie on my side for more than a few seconds. After towing or pumping sessions my hands felt as if they would never open fully again. There were times when there seemed to be no power at all in the fingers.

There had been moments when I wondered just how far the limits of human endurance could take me. Yet once those sea-boots were on my feet, none of the agony, the pain or the worry seemed to matter any more. If my feet were on the mend, then the rest of my body would catch up before long. The sea-boots and the westerly wind were exactly the ingredients for the tonic I needed. Maybe I looked a mess, maybe I was a mess, but I was on top once more and I didn't intend to fall off again.

That evening the sun showed itself and a following light rain shower created a huge rainbow which arched right across the sea and *Silver* was heading right through it. To me it was the gateway to home. Home! Harvest-time on the Venns' farm was not too far off. John had sent me a telegram before I left St Johns, saying: 'Don't forget to make it in time for the harvest.' I was now sure that I would do just that.

But how far? How long? How many more storms? How many more hours of rowing? And, more important, how many more chances would the Atlantic grant me?

This, however, was not the moment for cares or for thinking

of what might be. This was a moment to think of other things and there was plenty to think about—a walk in the hills, a beer with the lads, of things I had done, of things I hoped to do. All the good things, all the happy times. All the things which add up to a sailor's dream of home. I knew for sure that the fire was back in my belly at last. Nothing except final disaster could lick me now.

It occurred to me that up to now all my prayers on this trip had been a plea for help in moments of trouble. Surely now was the moment for a prayer of thanks. Heartfelt and humble thanks for the help which had reached me without being requested.

At five-thirty on the morning of Thursday, 10 July, I was wakened by the drone of a plane overhead. To me it was the sound of land. By the end of the day I realised that I was in an area where I would hear planes several times during the day and night. But two days passed without my being able to sight even a wing-tip. The grey cloudy skies had dogged me almost all the way were still with me. Yet I never failed to stare up-wards whenever I heard a plane, trying to follow the direction of the sound until it was out of earshot.

The days were passing with unflagging monotony. Wake up, eat, row, eat, row, tidy up *Silver*, pump, row, pump, sleep: over and over again the same routine, one day following an-other almost without change except for the speed of the wind. But my buoyant mood was still with me. It was going to take more than a spot of boredom to get me down from here on. I had worked out an estimated position on Saturday, 12 July. It was 52°06′N, 20°W. I made that just 720 miles from Ireland. The whiff of home was well and truly in my nostrils.

Sleep was out of the question. I was too excited for that. Whatever had happened, whatever could happen, I was sure I was going to make it. I had to do something and the only real exertion open to me was to row. I had rowed steadily through most of the day. Admittedly, I had been looking forward to supper and getting my head down. Now I could not bear the thought of missing a single valuable minute.

Throughout the night I stayed at the oars, rowing as if I would reach land by the morning. I stopped only for tea and a shot of rum at about 2 am. About an hour later I saw the lights of a ship heading east. Almost at the same moment I became aware of a shining ghostlike shape darting about in the water. I watched it switch from side to side of *Silver*. Apart from my tea breaks this was the only time I shipped my oars. I don't know how long I watched, but I think I was mesmerised for a while.

Then I realised it was a large fish glowing with the phosphorous which sparkled like tinsel glitter over the surface. I had no idea of what it was. Maybe, I thought, Bluey has returned to haunt me. But whatever it was, it was both beautiful and spooky. It hung around for about ten minutes and then suddenly vanished. One minute it was there bursting through the water like a shooting star, leaving dancing fire in its wake. The next second, nothing. I suppose it must have dived, having tired of its game with *Silver*.

For a few seconds I sat staring at the spot where it had disappeared. I was sorry to see it go, for those ten minutes had been quite the most beautifully entertaining of the trip. It had been like a cabaret show, made all the more welcome because it had been so unexpected. I was glad that I had decided to row through the night. And I rowed on.

By dawn I was bone weary, but I was happy. So happy, in fact, that my appetite returned in a rush. I breakfasted on porridge, tea and biscuits and marmalade, and then crawled into my shelter for a couple of hours' sleep.

A couple of hours was a complete underestimation. That night row had taken far more out of me than I had thought. I did not wake until three o'clock in the afternoon. Strangely enough, I couldn't have picked a better day to sleep if I could have forecast the weather ahead with pin-point accuracy.

It was a completely calm day. The Atlantic was barely ruffled by the mildest breeze. Yet even the term breeze is too strong to describe that peaceful day. Zephyr is the perfect word. The *Oxford Dictionary* defines it as 'the west wind personified'. How true, how true. Throughout the day it never blew harder than between two and three miles per hour, and I took full advantage of it. After a hurried meal I rowed through the afternoon until about five-thirty in the most perfect rowing conditions I had yet encountered. *Silver* and I fairly floated along.

And there was to be a perfect end to a perfect day. Just before five-thirty I spotted a ship which I thought might be the weather ship *Juliet* which was on station somewhere in the area I had entered. But she was steaming eastwards and was, I was sure, too far away to spot me. But this time I was taking no chances on being overlooked. It was the first ship I'd had a chance to stop and I was anxious to get a message to my friends back home.

I lit a flare and, standing on the seat, waved it above my head. But that ship showed no signs of seeing me. I tied a red anorak to the telescopic radio mast and raised it as far as it would go. Again there were no signs of recognition.

Then I fired one of my radar flares which rise to 2,000 feet and explode, shooting out a shower of fine metallic dust which should be picked up by a ship's radar. It worked. She changed course and bore down on me. As she steamed slowly past on my port side, there was a shout from the deck: 'Are you all right?' I yelled back: 'Yes, I'm okay. All I want is my position and to ask your skipper to radio a message back to Lloyd's in London.'

It was the S.S. *Hansa*, on her way to Deptford, London, with a cargo of newsprint for the Express Newspapers. I waved my chart above my head as she inched past me. Then the *Hansa* stopped and I rowed alongside. The captain climbed down from the bridge to the midships deck and shouted down: 'Your position is 52°24′N, 20°26′W.'

I scribbled it on a blank page in my log-book and then passed up my message and several rolls of films which I asked him to pass on to the *Sunday Express* when he got to Deptford. Then he asked if I wanted to come aboard, have a bath or just have a drink. I refused them all with thanks.

'How about food and water?' he shouted. 'Are you okay for supplies?'

'I am absolutely fine, thanks,' I shouted. 'I don't need a thing now I've got my position.'

With that the captain shouted: 'Okay. Keep clear of my propellers.' He gave me time to row off before starting his engines and heading for Blighty. I watched her for a few minutes, feeling a little wistful. But it did not last for long. When I checked the position he had given me I found I was only ten degrees from the Irish coast. And I made that no more than 600 miles.

The smell of the land was with me with a vengeance.

Meeting the S.S. *Hansa* left me with a most extraordinary bag of mixed emotions. I felt great, of course. I was still feeling great the next morning, Tuesday, 15 July. I couldn't feel anything else but great, knowing how close I was to success. But I wanted to talk to someone. You can get used to loneliness. But once it has been broken, no matter how briefly, that is when you begin to feel it.

I just wanted to talk to someone, anyone. I wanted to talk about the excitement of being only 600 miles from Ireland. I wanted to talk about how long those 600 miles would take to cover. In short, I wanted to talk about anything at all.

The funny thing is that when I'd had the chance with the *Hansa* alongside I'd almost waved them on their way, as if I'd wanted to get rid of them. Now it was too late, I remembered I had wanted to ask them for a time check; I had meant to ask them how the moon shot was getting along, I hadn't heard a thing since my radio packed up. And above all I had wanted to ask how John Fairfax was getting along.

As I thought of John, my mind raced back to that day a few weeks back when I had chosen him as my hate target; when I had beamed in on him to boost my all-important competitive spirit. I still wanted to beat him. Although I doubted that I now would, I was determined to try. But hate him? Not any more. How can you hate a man who is taking much the same chances as yourself? How could I hate a man who, for all I knew, might be dead?

If he was still at sea it was just a matter of time and luck holding out. I hoped it would for both of us. For me, at least, things were going very smoothly. The weather was still calm, the winds still westerly and still light. Life was as near perfect as it had been at any period during the trip.

Such a change in my fortunes deserved a toast. Out came the

rum bottle and I drank to my luck holding good for the rest of the voyage. 'Let it be smooth,' I said, 'and let it be quick.' And so it was, for a short while. The Atlantic behaved perfectly, as if apologising for past mischief. And how gracious that ocean was in its apologies.

Light northerly winds on Wednesday were just what I had wanted. I had been aiming to drop to the south a little and I couldn't have hoped for better conditions if I had been able to plan them. I rowed all day with a will and a spirit as buoyant as a rubber duck in a bath-tub.

I coasted along that day without a care in the world. Even the sun deigned to appear, albeit fleetingly, shyly peeping now and then from behind the white clouds overhead. Yet even without the sun it was a bright day. The sea was so clear and green that I would not have been surprised if I had discovered that it had emptied itself overnight and refilled with clean water.

For once the smell of the sea did not remind me of drying seaweed and rotting driftwood. For once it was the sort of aroma that had to be inhaled deeply, filling the lungs and re-charging the body with sharp, fresh and pure oxygen. I could taste the iodine, almost feel the ozone . . . in short I had, at last, fallen in love with the sea. It had become a friend that I felt could be trusted.

At nightfall the sea was once again a fairyland of phosphor-ous lights. It sparkled away as far as the eye could see. Each wave-top was a miniature city at night with street lamps and windows all ablaze, and as each little city disappeared there was another swooping gently upwards to take its place.

And just ahead of me *Silver*'s bows threw up sparks of dainty fire as she slid through the night towards the east. Surrounded, as I was, by one of nature's most beautiful moments it was easy to discount the tortured memories of the past few weeks as nothing more than a bad dream.

It was small wonder that by Thursday, 17 July, I found my-self actually singing once again. I think the cue for song came with the twelve jet liners which overflew me that day. I saw them all, some winging their way to the west, some winging in the same direction as *Silver* and myself.

How wonderful they looked as they threaded in and out of the clouds, leaving their vapour trails like brush-strokes across the patches of blue sky. No wonder I felt like singing. I could not remember all the lyrics, so I hopped from song to song, popping in the words where I could remember them and humming the rest. I ran through *Over the Sea to Skye, Danny Boy, Shoals of Herring* and *Wild Colonial Boy*. I strung them all together as if they were one song. I doubt very much if it sounded at all tuneful, for my voice sounds more like a cracked cup than anything else, but there was nobody to object and it made me feel great.

The last jet of the day flew by at about 6 pm. I had been wondering about the passengers in those planes all day. Where were they going? Did I, perhaps, know any of them? What would they have made of little *Silver* and myself if they could have seen us?

Maybe they were off on holiday, hopefully searching for sun and fun. Most of them would, no doubt, head for the nearest beach as soon as they reached their destination. I hoped that I would not land on a crowded holiday beach. There would be too much fuss and bother if they saw a wild-looking scarecrow trundling out of nowhere.

If I had the choice I'd have *Silver* pitch up on to the shelf of a remote and deserted sandy cove with just one little crofter's hut perched on the cliff above. But I had no choice. I would be more than happy to latch on to any piece of land which was kind enough to allow *Silver* to rest her weatherbeaten boards.

Even when the seas began to build up, my feeling of well-being was not interrupted. By 10 pm they were running high and heavy. I knew that I was facing another night of pumping sessions. I was right. An hour later I was on the pumps, but still undaunted. 'It is,' I grinned to myself, 'all part of the job.' In between those sessions I managed to snatch cat-naps, well alert now to the need to conserve my energy; to plan ahead even in moments of stress.

Sometimes in the morning—I didn't really know the time but I afterwards figured it must have been 2.30 am—I was in my shelter trying to snooze a little when it happened. In the very first frightening split seconds I thought I was a goner. Then there was no time to think of anything except survival.

There was a long rumbling crash and my little world literally turned upside down. I flung out my arms and feet in a frantic attempt to steady myself, but I was completely out of control. It happened so fast I didn't have time to figure out why, what or how. All I knew was that I was experiencing the most incredible sensation of spinning round inside my shelter rather like clothes in a washing machine.

Although I could not see in the darkness, I was most acutely conscious of being bumped around from floor to roof and from side to side, and all the while the loose articles in there were falling about me, on me and around me.

I had absolutely no idea of whether or not I turned once, twice or more. The overall impression was that I was being spun round and round in a locked cupboard. Even as I was going round, the sea was pouring in until I was utterly covered. It came in with such a rush that, in the confusion, I was sure that I had been swept overboard.

My eyes were shut and my cheeks extended to bursting point as I held my breath. It was so fantastically eerie to feel the water over my face and head, filling my ears and pressuring in between my clothes and body, that panic was merely a hair's-breadth away. It was the most chaotic and utterly bewildering moment of my life.

My arms and legs were still thrashing about as I fought to find something tangible in a world gone suddenly mad. My hand struck the canvas covering of my shelter. Sodden as it was and weighted by gallons of water, it seemed as heavy as lead. I wrestled with it, but did not seem able to shift it. 'Christ, oh my Christ!' . . . those words ran through my brain over and over again in desperate, frantic repetition.

Then I discovered that my heavy folded inflatable life-raft had jammed the free side of the canvas. The spinning had stopped by now and I was able to wrench it to one side and wriggle out of the shelter. I thought I'd had it—I was still under water. Then my head broke the surface.

There was just enough light for me to gaze with disbelieving eyes at the scene around me. *Silver* was completely filled with

water. And yet, incredibly defying all logic, she was still afloat
. . . just afloat. The fore and aft turtle decking was showing just
above the water, but the gunwales were about six inches under
the surface. I was sure that *Silver* was being held up only by the
buoyancy compartments, stuffed with blocks of polystyrene,
beneath that turtle decking.

I cursed at the top of my voice. I cursed the Atlantic the
weather, myself and my stupidity in ever starting out on this
trip, in a long string of savage, bitter oaths. In some odd way
the stream of filth propped me up—and I was badly in need of
some support. It was, I suppose, a show of bravado, for I had
been shaken to my very roots. If ever I was going to be frightened it was right then. Yet I knew I had no time to be frightened. I had to survive or die.

The priority was to get the water out of *Silver*. But how?
Although my baling bucket had been lashed down and was still
in place, I thought that such a conventional method would
take far too long. Then I had the bright idea of rocking the
water out of the boat.

I sat first on one gunwale amidships, pushing downwards
with all my weight until I could feel *Silver*'s side dipping slightly,
then moved quickly to the other side to catch it at the start of
the downward dip. I kept repeating this routine as quickly as I
could until I had *Silver* fairly rocking from side to side.

Gradually I managed to get each gunwale in turn to break
the surface. Then I cut the lashing on my baling bucket and, as
I continued to move from side to side, started heaving the water
out five gallons at a time. Slowly, so slowly it seemed like for
ever, each gunwale began to rock higher and higher above the
water. The progress was practically imperceptible, but eventually the water began to clear and the gunwales were no longer
under the water.

By the time *Silver*'s sides were about six inches above the
surface-level, I reckon I had managed to get rid of about a
quarter of the water. Then I sat on my rowing seat and began
baling like hell. I have no recollection of time, but by the time
I had got the water down to about six inches above the floorboards a new day was being born in the eastern sky.

It was Friday, 18 July, and I was alive to see it. I actually pinched myself to make sure. And then I prayed my eternal thanks as I baled. My feelings at the time can best be summed up in the words of John Millington Synge, the Irish dramatist, who in his book *The Aran Islands* wrote:

'A man who is not afraid of the sea will soon be drownded, for he will be going out on a day he shouldn't. But we do be afraid of the sea, and we do only be drownded now and again.'

Once *Silver*'s floorboards were clear of water, I turned to the pumps and worked at them non-stop until I heard the most welcome sound of them sucking on air. *Silver* and I were back in business, but what had brought us to the very brink of disaster?

It was the sea anchor. When in use the anchor, a sort of canvas bucket with no bottom which resists the push of wind and pull of current, drifts about thirty feet from the side of the boat. Normally it is secured by two ropes, one from the stem, the other from a cleat roughly halfway along the gunwale. The drag operating through these two ropes keeps boat and sea anchor in the correct position.

There was only one small piece of evidence for me to work on and I could only guess at what happened. I found that the shackle attaching the line to the stem had broken, thus leaving all the strain on the midships line, with *Silver* pivoting on that single rope like a swivel.

The sea must have turned *Silver* round so that this midships rope passed beneath her and concentrated all the strain of the dragging sea anchor on just one side of her. Then, I think, a strong or freak wave must have hit her on the opposite side to which that one rope was still fastened. That wave pitched her over in a big roll and that, combined with the pull of the rope underneath her, had been enough to roll her right over until finally she came right side up, but full of water.

I pulled in a few feet of the rope and made it fast round the forward samson post to ensure that the strain would be put upon the bows instead of amidships.

As I sat down for the first time in hours, I was panting for breath. My mouth lolled open and my eyes were closed as I sank back against the seat. I felt as weak as a wet paper handkerchief. Sweat poured from me in what was very nearly a cloud of steam. I was practically out for the count. Now that it was all over I just wanted to lie down.

Then the reaction set in. Beginning with a slight tremble which set every muscle twitching, it rapidly developed into a fit of the shakes which jerked my body from head to foot. Try as I would, the shakes could not be stopped. They obviously had to run their own course.

I don't know how long it lasted, but it seemed as if I would never be still again. I lay there letting my nerves play out their own little drama until I was finally somewhere near normal again and then I opened my eyes. It was like coming out of a long, dark, narrow tunnel. My throat was parched and my tongue felt swollen to twice its size. I wanted to gulp down pints, gallons of cold water. Instead I forced myself to sip slowly, first rinsing out my mouth, gargling and then allowing myself to swallow no more than a couple of mouthfuls.

Rowing was out of the question that morning. I would have to rest, no matter what happened. Yet I could not bring myself to crawl back into the shelter, which, for me, still represented a sort of chamber of horrors. The memory of the night's frantic turmoil was far too vivid. Still in the same clothes, still sopping wet, I propped my head up on one of *Silver*'s wooden ribs, curled up on the boards between the shelter entrance and my rowing seat and tried to sleep. It was a long, long time coming, but finally I drifted off into a blessed trouble-free sleep.

In the early hours of Saturday morning I awoke to yet another blustery bout of weather. It was coming in from the south-west at about 25 mph but caused me little discomfort. What really troubled me was the cold. The night air was eating into me. I was too exhausted to even think of covering myself and I was shivering again, but this time I knew only the weather was to blame.

There was one undeniable sign that my ducking had not caused any lasting effects. I was ravenously hungry. Then I realised I had not eaten a thing the day before. I had been without food or hot drink for nearly twenty-four hours.

Before I could prepare a meal I had to find my spare flashlight. The other must have been lost overboard in the upset, for I could not find it anywhere. Luckily the plastic box in

K

which the spare had been stowed had been firmly lashed down and, despite the fact that *Silver* had been totally swamped, the contents of the box were bone-dry.

Yet I had to wait just a little longer for my food. In the violence of the night before my cooker had been uprooted from the deck. The holding screws had been torn out of the floor-boards and the cooker had been flung to one side and jammed under a gunwale. I heaved a sigh of relief to see it lying there, dented, rusting, but still all in one piece. If that had gone over-board I would have been in a pickle. I screwed it to the deck once more.

What a banquet I had! Porridge with honey was the first course, sardines the second, and curry the main course. This was followed by canned fruit, marmalade, margarine and biscuits and a couple of Mars bars. I washed it down with a mug of instant coffee heavily laced with rum. And then, to celebrate my deliverance, I knocked back a large neat rum.

With the aid of the flashlamp I began the anxious task of checking over *Silver*. She was okay. There were absolutely no signs of a leak anywhere in her tough little frame. Then came the tidying-up session. Everything that was loose and by some peculiar chance still in the boat was wiped and lashed down. Everything that was lashed down was untied and re-lashed.

After that came the job of ensuring that the sea anchor was properly and firmly secured. That was quite a job. I crawled up on to the forward turtle decking, tucked a foot round the samson post and sprawled forward on my belly, wishing I had suction pads like a fly as *Silver* heaved about in the heavy swell.

I had to lean out and over the bow and tuck my head down as far as possible to get at the shackle bolt which was fixed about one foot down the stem. I had to use both hands to unscrew the shackle This was a laborious job which, in the dark, had to be handled with extreme care, as I did not want to lose that shackle—it was the only one I had.

Finally, after having to stop several times to stretch cramped muscles, I had the shackle unshipped, the end of the broken sea anchor rope re-spliced on to it and then screwed the shackle back into place. After that I bound the shackle and rope splice with wire in an effort to give it greater strength. The whole operation, which under normal circumstances would have taken no more than twenty minutes, took me close on an hour to complete. By the time I had finished I was aching with the strain of it, from head to toe. But that did not matter one jot. I felt happier that the job was done; happier because I felt more secure.

There was one last chore—a check on what was lost overboard during the Thursday-night upset. Strangely enough, it was not very much, but it was nevertheless damned annoying. One two-gallon container of drinking water was missing. Six days' supply of food, a kettle and a cup had gone. Also somewhere in the sea were all my charts except the main Atlantic one and one of the Irish coast. Not too bad at all, considering the mess I had been in. I still had food and water for a couple of weeks. *Silver* was still all in one piece, me too. What more did I need? What more could I ask?

12 | Sanctuary in Blacksod
20-27 July

If I had known, it still would not have seemed possible that this Sunday, 20 July, was the beginning of the last week of my Atlantic ordeal. Although by dead reckoning I made my position 52°N, 17°W—just about 400 miles to go—there was nothing tangible to go on; no signs of change; nothing to give me a hint.

Those leaden skies which had become so much a part of my everyday world were still glowering down from all points of the compass. And as always there was nothing to be seen but the racing, turbulent seas. That had been my daily scene for more than two months. I was so much a part of it by then that it was well-nigh impossible to comprehend any impending change.

Winds building up to 40 mph pounded into *Silver*, even now striving to drive her in the wrong direction. And she was far too light to be bounced about so freely. More than half of my food and water supplies had gone by this time and I had maintained a fair level of water in her bilges to prevent her riding too high in such a sea.

Trying to trim her in that sort of weather was, of course, virtually impossible, but as rowing was out of the question I was glad to have something else on which to concentrate. When I had managed to get her levelled off as much as I possibly could, I settled down to my Sunday letter.

It was from the quartermaster back at the SAS base in Hereford. He told me to 'stick at it'. Oh! brother, I had no option.

Silver and I stuck at it right through Monday's south-east winds and into a midday darkness of black threatening clouds which seemed to be heralding the end of the world. By dawn on Tuesday the wind decided to befriend me once again. Slanting in from due west it surged *Silver* along in gusts reaching about 30 mph. Working out a rough position, I placed myself at about 14°20'W. No more, it couldn't possibly be any more, than 240 miles left. I spent several hours at the oars, urging *Silver* towards that unseen coast.

Under such conditions the days began to speed by. The westerlies stayed with me, coaxing me along, nursing me, ushering me and all the time they seemed to be whispering: 'You're all right now. Do you hear? You're all right now. Don't worry any more. It's nearly over.'

Were they really being friendly? Or were they trying to lull me into a false sense of security? For it was not all plain sailing by a long chalk yet. From this point all the currents flowed northwards. Unless I took some counter-action, and tried to drop south a little, I could be swept away, missing the Irish and even the Scottish east coasts altogether. What a stupid ending that would be. But I was delighted to notice that I felt no anxiety about the situation. At long last my old cussedness was back at full strength and I was feeling as stubborn as a mule.

Thursday, 24 July, dawned like a public holiday. The sun I'd yearned for and so seldom seen came out with a vengeance. By 11 am the paintwork of my shelter roof was too hot to touch. I wallowed in the sunshine like a happy hippopotamus. I stripped to my swimming shorts, washed down in a bucket half full of cold clear drinking water and revelled in it all. Salt sores, blisters, aching joints, bruised muscles? What did I care about such trivialities? To blazes with them all. I could feel new life surging through my body. When I thought of Shackleton and his men spending eighteen months in the Antarctic I felt ashamed of my petty complaints about two months in the Atlantic.

A sight of that Irish coast was all I needed to make that the perfect day. Where, oh where was that Irish coast? Wherever it might be I was utterly sure that I could smell it and what a wonderful smell it was. As if to convince me, jet planes appeared about twenty miles to my north and still rising, as if they had not fully completed their take-off. That surely could mean only one thing: I couldn't be too far off Shannon and its international airport. Maybe it was imagination, but I don't think I had ever rowed quite so well since I had left St Johns. Apart from meal breaks, I rowed steadily until 10 pm. Then I slept like a baby.

The wind had swung against me by the morning of Friday, 25 July. It came swinging in from the south-east, absolutely the opposite to what I wanted and needed. Long before midday it had built up to near 50 mph and put paid to any hope of rowing. In a desperate bid to keep *Silver* from being driven too far to the north-west, I heaved two sea anchors overboard and from then on could only hope they would do the trick.

As *Silver* and I sat it out, two fishing boats appeared ahead of me about two miles away. They obviously had not spotted me and were too far away for me to hail. For a brief moment I dickered with the idea of sending up a flare. But I let them go without bothering them. I must confess my decision not to attract their attention was partly governed by doubts about my ability to resist an offer of a tow or help in some way. I had made it so far on my own. That had been the plan and it had to be played out until the bitter end or I would betray myself.

Judging from the appearance of those fishing boats, I figured I had three or maybe four more days to go. It was time to get my emergency landing kit ready. Into an empty waterproof flare container went my log-books, food rations, medical kit, some small hand flares, my camera and some rolls of film which I had taken on the trip. But fate was due to be kinder than I had given her credit for. My calculation of three or four days was woefully astray.

A steaming cup of coffee at six-thirty on the morning of Saturday, 26 July, set me up for what I thought would be just another day. It certainly began as such. Then things started happening. At nine-thirty I spotted a ship off my starboard beam. Although I tied my anorak to the telescopic radio aerial, she failed to spot me. Shortly after ten o'clock far away to the east a long, low, dark shadow appeared on the horizon. Could it be Ireland. I stared at it for quite a while, but it changed shape and then slowly disappeared. Disappointedly, I told myself it must have been a cloud or smoke from a ship.

The next hour and a half passed without incident. There was very little wind and I rowed steadily to the south-east. At eleven-thirty I threw a glance over my shoulder and stopped rowing.

It was land, land, land. I had just seen, positively beyond all doubt, land for the first time in over two months.

There was absolutely no doubt at all about it this time. This was not shadow, cloud or smoke. This was the real McCoy. It could not be too far away either. I reckoned it would take eight hours to reach, just eight hours. I wanted to dance. Instead I just yelled with delight.

For two more solid hours I rowed to the south-east. Over a coffee break I took a look at my chart of the Irish coast. I was sure I was off the Mullet Peninsula of County Mayo in northern Eire. But how far now? A quick estimation gave me ten miles to go. A mere ten miles after more than 2,000! Bursting with excitement, I rowed on and on. At three-thirty a fishing trawler called the *Ebba Victor* came steaming towards me. Curious fishermen stared at me. 'Are you all right?' they called.

'All right?' I replied. 'I'll say I'm all right. Never been better.' Then I pointed to the land and asked: 'Is that Mullet?'

'It is,' they replied. I waved my thanks and turned back to my oars. I wondered if they would ask me if I needed a tow. That was the last thing I needed right then. But they didn't. Without another word they steamed off about their own hazardous business.

At five o'clock I stopped for tea and a reconsideration of my previous calculations. It was taking longer than I had thought it would to get to that coastline. My guess of eight hours and then ten miles had been way off beam. Half an hour later the wind was strengthening from the south and pushing me away from the land. Perhaps it was just as well at that moment. From what I could make out the coast was treacherously rocky. White foam was boiling along the edge. It was a pretty hairy sight.

The wind started edging round to the west, setting me on a fair easterly course, but not head-on to land. It came at the right time, for it gave me a chance to look for a suitable landing spot—a sandy beach or a river entrance—before darkness fell.

I had still not spotted what I needed by 10 pm. By then I was four to five miles off a rocky headland, trying to slide down-wind and aiming to get behind that rock mass, as I was sure I would at least find shelter from the weather there. I fought hard to make it, but the wind grew too strong for me.

I knew right then I was not going to make it that night. I certainly did not want to take the risk of landing in the dark. By 1 am the wind and sea had swept me right past that headland. I grimly settled down to an all-night session at the oars, paddling away to keep me off those damned rocks. The Atlantic was not going to let me get away from her too easily.

A little earlier I had spotted what I took to be the glow of a lighthouse beam. It had showed faintly away to the north-east. As I headed *Silver*'s nose out to sea to maintain a safe distance from the land, I kept a look-out for that beam. I saw it sharp and clear at 2 am. But my work was still hard labour. The wind had swung round to the south and running at about 30 mph. I had no alternative but to keep *Silver* heading north. Within a short time I could see that I was at the entrance of what appeared to be a large bay.

It was now or never. I headed into the centre of the bay, rowing like mad to escape the pull of the wind. Slowly, gruelling stroke after stroke, I edged in until I was actually getting some protection from the land. It was much easier from then on. Shortly after 3 am dawn began to lighten the sky and I made a beeline for the lighthouse. I knew I was off Mullet but did not know exactly where, and this was not the time to look, for the wind was almost dead astern of me.

Silver drew closer to the lighthouse with agonising slowness and by four-thirty it was light enough for me to see a great range of rocks beneath it. It was going to be a tricky, even dangerous, landing. My main chance, I decided, was to grab my landing kit ready to jump clear as *Silver* humped up on to those rocks. I didn't want to see her smashed to pieces, but there was no alternative. I couldn't go on looking for a soft sandy beach for ever. If I was going to get ashore it had to be now.

There was just a few yards to go whan I made a quick check on my wrist-watch. It was five-thirty. Seconds later *Silver* hit with a juddering bump. The water was boiling beneath her, heaving her up, and the noise of the surging surf was almost deafening. I have to admit I did not spare any thoughts for

Silver. I was in the air, leaping towards the rocks, at almost the identical moment she struck.

I staggered, bumped my right knee, and straightened just in time for the next incoming wave to knock me right off balance. The water carried me onward and upward to a higher ledge of the rock.

I wallowed about there on my backside like a stranded porpoise, then scrambled back to my feet. Looking down, I could see *Silver* being pounded on the jagged edges of a stepped, slab-like formation of rocks. She had turned broadside on and was in imminent danger of being smashed.

Watching her surging back and forth on those rocks I felt as guilty as hell. How could I let her down after all she had meant to me; after the magnificent performance she had given? I just could not leave her there like that while I headed for safety. We had come through it all together. We should be safe together.

Even as I thought about it I was moving towards her. I slung my landing kit on board and jumped into the water up to my chest. I had to get *Silver* off those rocks. I got my shoulder under her bow and manhandled her nose out into the water again. It took nearly an hour to do it and all the time we were both being pushed, pounded and pummelled by that tormenting sea.

But we made it. Once I had her bow on to the sea I managed to hold her steady long enough to wait for the next receding wave and as *Silver* began to slip out with it I jumped aboard.

Frantically I unshipped a pair of oars, slammed them into the rowlocks and started to row like mad. For nearly half an hour we moved so slightly that we were almost at a standstill. There were times when my oars struck the rocks just beneath us. But finally I got her moving. I got her out about 250 yards, past the spit of rocky shore on which the lighthouse stood and round to the other side of the rocks.

Suddenly everything was dead calm. The force of the wind had been cut almost to nil as I rocked gently in the shelter of the rocks and stared at the scene ahead of me. I could not believe my eyes. There was a large sandy cove with hundreds of yards of gently shelving beach as soft as a baby's bottom. My dream landing had come true. There was not a soul in sight.

Slowly I pulled to that marvellous, wonderful, glorious, peaceful beach. I kept pulling until *Silver* nosed her way on to the sand and I did not stop until she was stuck tightly, safely and cosily. We had made it. It was 7 am on Sunday, 27 July, 1969. I jumped out, heaved her as far up on the beach as I could and tied a rope round a large boulder. Then I stood and looked at her. For the first time I realised I was actually standing on dry land. And my legs felt firm, not a sign of the wobbles which I had believed would hit me.

Looking at *Silver*, I was overwhelmed with pride and affection for her. She had truly become a part of me. Suddenly I realised she looked a bit of a mess. I couldn't leave her like that exposed to the eyes of strangers. I pulled as much of the sea grass as I could off her hull, then scrubbed her down with an old brush. Then jumping aboard I squared away everything until she was as shipshape as possible; until she could feel respectable.

As I headed for the roadway above the beach I felt as lively as a cricket. Standing in the doorway of a nearby cottage was an elderly woman who had obviously seen me land on the beach. I waved at her and called out: 'Good morning, ma'm. I've just rowed the Atlantic. Can I take your photograph?'

She, quite obviously, thought I was utterly mad. Edging back into her house, she shook her head. Before she disappeared I asked: 'Then can you please tell me where I am?'

I caught her reply just before she closed her front door. I had come home to Blacksod Bay, County Mayo.

Now all I needed was sleep . . . deep, undisturbed sleep. Just 400 yards away I spotted the only pub in that tiny village. I stepped out towards it.

Appendix
What it takes to row the Atlantic

The boat

20 ft Yorkshire dory, 5 ft 6 in. beam constructed from Thames
  Marineply

Modifications
Hull sheathed with nylon cascover
Turtle decking front and rear with bulkheads
Hand rail to samson post
Gunwale raised 9 in. in oak
Buoyancy compartments fore and aft
Overhead cover gunwale to gunwale
Water store under false floor

Equipment
2 Henderson bilge pumps
Davey sea anchors
3 pairs ash oars 9 ft long
Safety harness and 20 ft nylon rope
200 ft rope
Nylon cord (various sizes)
Maintenance list
12 elastic bonges
Monsanto polystyrene buoyancy cubes
Thermometer (for water temperature)
Knives and knife sharpener
Ensign
3 waterproof torches
Marlin spike

Navigation

Kelvin Hughes sextant
Stopwatch

2 Seiko wrist-watches
Sestrel ship's compass
Parallel rulers
Dividers (single-handed)
Binoculars
Log-books
Hard black pencils and sharpener
Time signals WWV 2.5; 5; 10; 15 mcs.

Charts
North Atlantic (ghreomic)
All routine North Atlantic charts for May, June, July, August,
September

Books
Reed's Pilot Books: Western Ireland; South West England
AD List of Lights, British Isles
2 volumes Computed Altitude and Azimuth 1969

Safety

One man RAF life-raft
Self-inflating life-jacket
Schermuly flares
Fog-horn with refills
Three 3 ft parachute-type drogues (sea anchor)
Heliograph
10 in. radar reflector
Deep-sea fishing line

Communications

Hacker Helmsman transistor radio
SARBE Beacon (Mark II) 2182 (emergency)
Clifford & Snell Lifeline radio

Photography

Waterproof 35 mm Pentaflex camera
Kodak film (30 black and white, 10 colour)

Special long cable release
Camera rigged to fit several anchoring positions

Clothing

8 teeshirts
8 sets underclothes
3 polar suits
2 nylon ski suits
3 Peter Storm sailing suits
8 sweaters
7 pairs Army trousers
20 pairs socks
1 pair shorts
1 pair Dunlop Wellingtons
3 towels
1 Balaclava
1 floppy hat
3 pairs gloves
2 pairs sunglasses
1 rubber repair outfit

Bedding

4 space blankets (retain 80 per cent body heat)
1 sleeping bag
2 Lilos

Medical

A Traveller's Guide to Health by Lieutenant-Colonel James M.
   Adam
Glucose tablets
Morphine tablets and surettes
Codeine tablets
Seasickness tablets
Penicillin tablets
Tetracyclin tablets (boils)
Vitamic C tablets (boils)
Chalk opium tablets

Surgical spirit
Vaseline
Calamine compound (salt sores)
Barrier/antiseptic cream
Lanoline
Paraffin gauze (boils)
Surgical kit
Cotton wool
Butterfly dressings
Plasters
Lint
Bandages (gauze and crepe)

Washing

Soap
Face towel
Shaving kit and Gillette blades
Mirror
Body powder
Combs
Maclean's toothpaste
2 toothbrushes
Ear kit
Dental kit

Food and drink

100 SAS packs (dehydrated food, vitamin and iron pills, tea,
    coffee, etc.)
Polythene bags (300-gauge) for packing food
Tupperware containers
Two weeks' fresh rations
20 days' Horlicks storm rations
100 galls water in 2-gallon polythene bags
Water-sterilising tablets
Clorex
Tree Top fruit squash

Solar still
Jerry-can with tap on bottom (for water)
60 cans Whitbread's beer
10 bottles Navy Neaters Rum
Wrigley's Chewing Gum
4 jars of curry paste and assorted 'goodies' from Tesco
Maxwell House coffee
Cadbury's Smash
Tetley tea bags

Cooking equipment

Bleuet Camping Gaz stove (with specially built shield)
Prestige pressure cooker
2 kettles
Plastic mug
Spoons
Waterproof matches

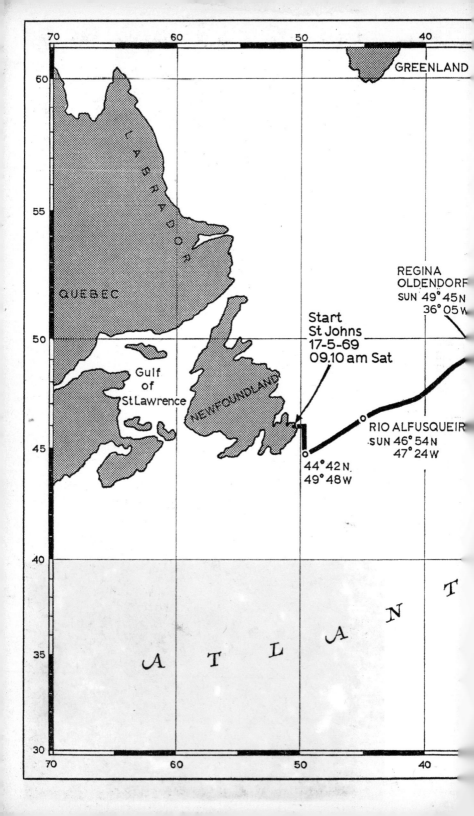